46316

Knowledge and wisdom, far from being one,
Have oft times no connection. Knowledge dwells
In heads replete with thoughts of other men:
Wisdom in minds attentive to their own.
Knowledge is proud that he has learn'd so much;
Wisdom is humble that he knows no more.

WILLIAM COWPER

Toward Excellence in College Teaching

TOWARD
EXCELLENCE

IN COLLEGE
TEACHING

Earl V. Pullias and Aileene Lockhart
University of Southern California

Marjorie H. Bond
Southern Illinois University

Marguerite Clifton
University of California, Los Angeles

Donna Mae Miller
University of Arizona

WM. C. BROWN COMPANY PUBLISHERS
135 SOUTH LOCUST STREET · DUBUQUE, IOWA 52003

Manufactured by WM. C. BROWN CO. INC., Dubuque, Iowa
Printed in U. S. A.

Preface

Although we cannot begin to express the appreciation we feel nor repay the debts we owe, there are certain acknowledgments which must be made. It is impossible and unnecessary to trace to their origin our ideas and ideals about teaching and learning. The most important things known or believed about education have become a part of the heritage of man. Individual writers can hope to do little more than reflect this knowledge and belief from the mirror of their minds, and thus perhaps cast them in a new perspective and maybe add a slightly different dimension to them. In preparing this book we have been appreciatively aware of those who have taught us (or tried to teach us) in the past: teachers, colleagues, students, writers, known and unknown. All have contributed, yet as is the nature of life we must take full responsibility for what finally appears here.

The following publishers and copyright holders have kindly given us permission to use quoted materials:

American Psychological Association, William F. Buckley Jr., Norma Millay Ellis, Mrs. Roswell L. Gilpatric, *Harper and Brothers, Harper and Row, Harper's Magazine, Harvard University Press, Hillman Periodicals, The Journal of Educational Sociology,* Kudner Agency, *J. B. Lippincott Company, The Macmillan Company, New Haven: College and University Press, New York University Press, Penguin Books, Princeton University Press, Saturday Review, Southern Illinois University Press, Time, University of Redlands Alumni Magazine,* and *John Wiley and Sons.*

We wish to express appreciation to many patient friends and relatives who have critically read the manuscripts, assisted with typing, helped with the arduous chore of proofreading, and in many other ways strengthened our hands.

Finally, a word should be said about division of labor in this cooperative effort. The actual authorship is indicated on the individual chapters. However, by mutual agreement the coauthor (Dr. Aileene Lockhart) accepted the heavy responsibility of editing the volume. It was her task, in addition to writing the chapters that bear her name, to bring all the material into such unity as it has achieved, not infrequently by rewritings and additions. Also, she had responsibility for the numerous routine activities that are involved in bringing a book to press. Her colleagues in this endeavor deeply appreciate both her spirit and skill.

1964 — The Authors

Contents

PART ONE

The Roots
of Excellence

Introduction:
The Creative Spirit

Aileene Lockhart

The story is told by a favorite pupil and assistant of Rodin.[1] It tells of the birth of THE THINKER, the great sculptured figure which Rodin wished to stand before the Pantheon, a figure not to honor warriors but "the artists and statesmen, the lovers and thinkers, the illustrious of France."

...But think as he might, no proper conception for the statue came to Rodin. Tables, benches, chairs, the floor itself, were covered with drawings, with clay questings of his unsatisfied spirit. He had dismissed with a moment's scorn the obvious theme: no Greek sage solemn in his robe, no earnest philosopher with a papyrus scroll. For some years no work had thus dwelled within him, thus wrung him with travail of its creation. In all the restlessness and unapproachable impatience of those hard months—hard for him and for us who were working with him—

---

[1]From *AUGUST RODIN* by Victor Frisch and Joseph T. Shipley. Copyright 1939 by J. B. Lippincott Company. Published by J. B. Lippincott Company.

1

there was a sense once more of truly germinal chaos out of which new beauty would be born.

And one afternoon he came from the private corner of the studio, the deep lines that had marked his inner struggle smoothed away, his familiar, friendly smile a-twinkle in his eyes.

"Let's go and eat!" was all he said. But THE THINKER, though as yet invisible, had taken form.

As usual, Rodin made a large number of little clay figures, comparing, constantly changing, then destroying all but one. At last he called us in, drew quick drawings of the projected statue, front, back and both profiles, and set us to building the armature. It was to be twelve times the size of his sketches.

When Rodin had checked and approved our work, we laid on the clay, following the drawings as closely as we could. Even from them, we were aware of the magnitude and daring of his conception; and we worked in a fever of joyous expectancy. When the rough outlines of the figure were visible, Rodin dismissed us and locked the studio door. It was seven months before any other than he stepped inside.

I was in the stable tending to Nancy, the master's twenty-eight-year old mare. . . .He hurried over and asked how Nancy was faring. . . .And I watched the inspired sculptor in him slip away as just an aging old man stroked his dear friend, the aged horse.

It was only the next morning that we looked upon THE THINKER, the majestic figure that is a monument to thought's first struggling into the emergent brain, to man's evolving out of brute, to the primeval ancestor of all the seers and sages.

. . .Whenever possible, and whether the finished figure was to be marble or bronze, Rodin would have the plaster cast erected where the statue was to stand, and study its proportions and harmonies as affected by the surroundings. Early in the morning, with two loaded carts, we set out from Meudon for the Pantheon. Four of us pulled and pushed the handcart that bore the cast; two walked alongside to guard against its rolling. And four others brought the material for the base, ladders, boards, shellac, bronze dust and other equipment. The day was darkening before we had finished coloring the erected cast; we covered it with canvas, went for dinner, then back to Meudon. The next day, Rodin would study the figure in its environment; then it would be loaded on the cart once more, and brought back to Meudon.

. . .In the next day's downpour of rain, we took the train to the city. As we hurried from the Gare des Invalides to the Pantheon, we could see from afar that the silhouette under the canvas had changed. What incredible thing had occurred?

From beneath the canvas a great sliding of broken and crumbled plaster lay around. On removing the cover, we found THE THINKER smashed into thousands of pieces. A policeman, now on hand, informed us that some twenty students from the Academy, caught when a larger number fled, were under arrest for the outrage. Pupils of Rodin's arch enemies, they had swept upon the figure with their cudgels, and demolished it. Had Rodin, like their masters, been in the habit of resting content with the first modeling, and ordered but one cast, their work would have been indeed a devastation.

The sculptor smiled grimly: "The Academy, which is death, cannot destroy THE THINKER, who is life."

And in four days another cast, set up and guarded during the night awaited Rodin's study in the morning.

But that night, more than he grieved over the Academy's envy, Rodin mourned the death of Nancy, his aged mare.

No teacher can read this story and fail to find in it many answers to the excellence which is sought widely on every hand today. What is the "more" that makes for excellence—excellence in teaching, excellence in the techniques of good thinking, excellence in perspective and balance, excellence in humanness? What does excellence require? Obvious are the spirit and tenacity, the questing, the dissatisfaction with anything not one's best, the working habits of a seeker of surpassing goodness, the patience and the bearing of disappointment, the tenderness and compassion of a great man.

And what things mediate against excellence? Examples here include deep rooted jealousies, vicious reprisals, and the sterility of the Academy. How damning the implication that the Academy is devoted to dead knowledge, that its members are not only content with the *Status Quo Ante*, jealously resenting superiority not in its inner circle, but also actually being party to the destruction of the creative outside its ranks. No teacher can read these words without thought: "The Academy, which is death, cannot destroy The Thinker, who is life."

Society, we believe, desperately demands a great number of devoted and dedicated persons who can utilize not only the best of the accumulated knowledge of the past but also stimulate the search for new discovery and knowledge. Devastating indeed is a literal interpretation of Rodin's words, and tragic indeed in any case where they be true.

The present little volume is a symposium of ideas and opinions, the result of the thinking of five persons (plus our indebtedness to many), all college and university teachers for a number of years. Disturbed by the problems, the responsibilities, and the obligations of higher education—but with "joyous expectancy" convinced of its possibilities—we have attempted to examine critically the purposes of higher education and some means to attain these purposes. We have tried to forget completely about traditional teaching-learning patterns, about trivial daily problems, about filling this-or-that gap. We have endeavored to start from scratch: What is higher education about? What is the role of higher learning in a free society? What makes certain colleges and universities true places of higher learning? What pathways lead to excellence?

We are concerned for our students—what they are LIKE, what we believe they should KNOW, how we want them to FEEL, how they can learn to THINK, what they must be able TO DO, what we hope they will STRIVE FOR. These are questions we have asked ourselves: How can we develop the value judgments, the critical and creative thinking so necessary for our time—abilities which may well provide answers to the great question marks of our era? What qualities do effective teachers have that thrust their students forward with initiative and eagerness toward widening horizons, to forever search for truth and beauty?

It seems to us that the higher education has sat on the fence about as long as it is going to hold. Our purposes must be clearer. We must be COMMITTED to something. What really is central in education? To what end should we teach? What and why and how are we teaching? No longer can we be "watchdogs over our own little plots." This little book is the result of our efforts to understand what higher education can be, AT BEST, and to explore ways of developing the acquisitive and inquisitive mind in a framework of deep respect for human personality.

Higher Education in Modern Society

Earl V. Pullias

Higher education carries a heavy responsibility in modern society. No institution has greater opportunities to contribute significantly to the upward movement which modern man must achieve. Higher education at its best is the only institution in modern society that is free to seek answers to all the problems that confront man, through the use of every method the mind of man can conceive. By its very nature the primary allegiance of higher education is to truth: its discovery, its wide dissemination, and its effective application to the questions of life. Thus, in theory, colleges and universities have no vested interests that would influence either ends or means. Their task is the full exploration of the nature of all phases of reality—a free, never-ending search that ranges from the nature of a grain of sand or a leaf to the nature of love or faith or Ultimate Reality.

This process involves essentially two things. Higher education passes on to the rising generation that which man has learned from his experience on this planet. This rich achievement has been deposited chiefly in the records of man's behavior, most clearly perhaps in books, but also in objects such as buildings, tools, and instruments. The results of experience are apparent also in organizations, institutions, and complex customs. It may be that the richest ore in the deposit of experience is living language. Indeed every language symbol is a concentrate of almost limitless experience. All of these records or deposits taken together are the culture of man.

Higher education proposes to give young men and women the benefit of that long and rich experience. Thus to transmit the culture is to enable the new generation to profit from all man has learned. The first responsibility is, in Ortega's phrase, to bring those educated "to the height of the times,"[1]* which means to understand and live in terms of the best mankind has learned. This transmission of the culture is not a passing on of dead knowledge, attitudes, and processes. As Professor Whitehead has so vividly pointed out, the transmission, to be effective, must be the "imaginative consideration of learning," essentially a creative uniting of the spontaneity of youth with the discipline and caution of age.

The second large task of higher education is search and discovery. Although man has had a long and profitable experience, he has learned very little about reality. As Newton said about his achievements, "I do not know what I may appear to the world; but to myself I seem to have been only like a boy playing on the seashore, and diverting myself in now and then finding a smoother pebble or a prettier shell than ordinary, whilst the great ocean of truth lay all undiscovered before me." The spirit of the higher learning is this free, unceasing search for new truth.

Throughout the process of transmission (described in the foregoing), the unfettered spirit of inquiry is central. Every previously established fact, every insight suggested by prophet, seer, poet, scientist, or magician is imaginatively and critically considered in the all-engaging spirit of search and research. Thus by constantly throwing all previously known things into new combinations and by skillful probing through intuition or experimentation into the unknown, error is corrected and new truth is discovered.

Here then we have a beginning conception of the nature and purpose of higher education: to assist man to learn the essence of what has been learned up to now; and to continue the search for additional truth, embedding in those who have the experi-

---

*[1]Superior numbers refer to references cited by chapter beginning on page 128.

ence of the higher learning the humble but fearless spirit of end-
less inquiry. Of course, colleges and universities are not the only
places where teaching and research go on, but these processes are
the prime opportunity and responsibility of higher education.
Wherever these things take place with zest and in freedom, there
the spirit of the higher learning, the idea of the university, exists
and does its incomparable work.

Throughout the history of man, the experience of the higher
learning has been limited to a very small proportion of the population. Professor Arnold Toynbee suggests that this limitation
was often deliberate in order to reserve the specific benefits for
a particularly select group, often from a given social class, extended occasionally to the highly gifted of other classes.[2] This
ancient doctrine of the elite was usually rationalized by the argument that only those of very special ability and background
could profit from higher education.

In a sense the argument was sound and indeed continues to be
sound, for the higher learning experience was mediated through
a vocabulary and special skills available to only a highly
privileged group. Thus a circular process became established
that inevitably upheld the arguments which were used to support
the limitation of educational opportunity: only those of the privileged class had the opportunity to learn the skills and the attitudes of mind which enabled them to partake in the critical and
imaginative consideration of the heritage of the race. All others
(except a specially gifted and strongly motivated few) either
had no opportunity or incentive to partake of the process or,
when they attempted it, failed and thus supported the primary
argument on which the theory of limitation was based.

It is interesting and, in a sense, frightening to note that this
situation continues to exist in nearly all nations of the modern
world. I believe that this condition is the most fundamental obstacle to the development of a genuinely modern world civilization that might face and eventually solve some of man's most
urgent problems.

The philosophy of severely limiting the higher education experience continued in full force in the United States until after
the War Between the States, although a new spirit had been
struggling toward birth in the work of Franklin, Jefferson,

Eliphalet Nott, Wayland, Horace Mann and others.[3] After 1865, there were great developments both in theory and practice which opened higher education to more and different people. The land grant college movement, the work of White at Cornell, Angell at Michigan, Eliot at Harvard, the development of normal schools which grew into state colleges, the rapid growth of the "hill-top" church-related college, the evolution of the great Midwestern state universities, and especially the concept and growth of the junior college comprised a far-reaching and basically new approach to higher education.

The doctrine of the elite designed to limit educational opportunity at the college and university level was contrary to the essence of the American vision for man and society. This great experiment in democracy could not be given a fair trial until a new educational philosophy had come into being and had been put into practice. This meant that higher education must be made available to all the people who could profit from it, without regard for social and cultural background or special notions of ability. But the concept of the nature of higher education and who could profit from it had been thousands of years in growing. The limiting point of view and practices were embedded in custom, law, institutions, and even language. No departure that the American Republic undertook has required more profound changes in both thought and practice.[4] It therefore should be no mystery that the goal of making higher education available to a wide variety of the population has really never been accepted as a sound philosophy nor put fully into practice.

Nevertheless, great strides have been made and the struggle still rages. Although remnants of the doctrine of the elite may yet be observed in considerable force everywhere in this society, not least within the ranks of higher education itself, a steadily increasing number and proportion of American young people want to go to college and actually go.[5] That is, the magnificent process of the higher learning is opened up to more and more people, most of whom, at any other time or place in the history of mankind, would not have had this opportunity.

College teachers will be interested in a few statistics about college and university enrollment. First, gross enrollment figures:

according to the United States Office of Education,[6] the total enrollment for credit in the fall semester was as follows for these years: 1939—1,364,815; 1949—2,456,841; 1959—3,402,297; 1960—3,610,000. A conservative estimate for 1970 is 7,000,000. Even more interesting figures show the proportion of college age youth who were taking some college work in the years mentioned. Of the young people 18-21 years of age in the United States, the following percentages were taking some work in college: 1939—14.2; 1949—27.2; 1959—36.2; 1960—37.2.

These facts reflect a profound revolution in attitude and practice in higher education. They are a part of one of the most significant experiments in the history of man. In essence, they suggest that the United States is determined to open up the experience of the higher learning (the transmission of the heritage and the urgent spirit of inquiry) to all of its people who can profit from the process. Further, higher learning is being studied carefully to find changes that might make it more profitable to those of high or special ability and of different levels and types of ability.

These developments have the most profound implications for all the activities of colleges and universities, and especially for the work of the college and university teacher. This new approach to the higher learning demands new attitudes and new skills in the teacher. The purpose of this book is to assist the college teacher to reach maximum effectiveness in meeting the special responsibilities of modern higher education.

2

The Role of the College Teacher

Earl V. Pullias

The Meaning of Excellence

The term excellence is being so loosely used and so overused at present that its basic meaning is threatened. It has become a fad to talk about excellence and its pursuit. Certainly not all that has been written or said recently about this great quality, however, has been pretense or a verbal substitute for meaningful action. Teachers may find the following items helpful, for they are thoughtful and responsible: John W. Gardner, *Excellence;*[1] Louis T. Benezet, "The Trouble with Excellence;"[2] Edith Hamilton, *The Echo of Greece.*[3]

Excellence in teaching means the inclination and the ability to do with high skill the work of a teacher; that is, to play effectively the role of the teacher in the process of learning. Such excellence depends on a clear and developing concept of that role, personality traits of a special order, much professional knowledge, many highly developed skills, and a particular art that expresses itself in a personal style. Excellence as used here thus has special meaning: namely, doing effectively a very complex job. Every good teacher longs to grow in excellence in this sense.

This excellence of which we speak is not a meaningless thing. The power of the effective college teacher is very great. He has a creative relation with personality when childhood has been left behind and adulthood has not yet been reached, a period when there is often much fluidity or flexibility in the personality. Contact with a great teacher at this time in one's life in the setting of a college or university will often shape the whole direction and tone of the student's life. A bad experience in these years may block and distort further development.

I am aware that much of the research evidence seems to indicate that the impact of the college experience is in many cases not great, particularly on character.[4] The significance of this evidence is not clear; it may mean that George Williams' bitter contention, in *Some of My Best Friends Are Professors*,[5] that most of college teaching is very badly done, is correct. But whatever the meaning of this type of evidence, it can in no way negate the cloud of personal witnesses to the power and influence of great teachers. Accounts of such influence abound from Plato to the present. References may interest the college teacher: Houston Peterson's *Great Teachers*;[6] Gilbert Highet's chapter on "Great Teachers" in *The Art of Teaching*;[7] *College in a Yard*,[8] edited by Brooks Atkinson; and a special favorite of mine, *Teacher*,[9] by Helen Keller.

Immediately the question arises as to whether anything can be learned that will significantly improve the teacher. In short, is the great teacher born and not made? Certainly this is a complex question that only the ignorant would spurn or answer lightly. Doubtless inherent qualities of personality and character contribute to or limit skill in teaching. Such qualities evidently are complex and appear in an infinite variety of combinations; thus they remain largely unknown in spite of much research in the area. These traits set the groundwork for skill in teaching and profoundly influence what may be called the art or style of teaching which, as already stated, is a highly personal matter.

But there is a science aspect of teaching which involves a great deal of knowledge—things that can and must be learned if one would achieve excellence in teaching. A suggestion of some areas where knowledge is basic to excellence may be helpful. Among other things, the great teacher must know much of (1) the psychology of himself and others; (2) the nature and meaning of the educative process at the college level; (3) the needs, interests, and abilities of the youth with whom he works; (4) the particular area of human experience (the subject and related disciplines) which he proposes to mediate through teaching. Evidently much can be learned by formal study about these things. However, just as a comparable knowledge on the part of a doctor or a lawyer does not make a great practitioner, so such knowledge, as important as it may be, does not alone make a great teacher.

I have little faith in tricks, devices, or gimmicks that put in a list may appear to be helpful, but which really do little or nothing to improve teaching. Certainly an effective teacher learns many "how to's" or practical tricks of his trade; however, to be meaningful they must be his own, developed in terms of his own personality and experience, and based upon sound and clearly understood principle. The teacher will find no practical do's and don't's in this discussion, rather some relatively simple principles that may be useful in the guidance of growth. These principles grow out of the thought and research found in the large and growing literature on college teaching and college learning.[10] Due to the nature and purpose of this book there is a minimum of documentation. References are given only when additional reading would likely interest and help the practicing teacher.

The Role of the Teacher

The question here is, "What must the excellent modern teacher be able to do well?" Clearly this question is extremely complex, and a full answer, if it could be given, would require a wide-ranging discussion of every phase of the educational endeavor. It is not my purpose to undertake such an answer, but to state very simply the basic tasks that must be performed by every teacher. If these are satisfactorily done the teacher will be an adequate teacher; if they are done with a measure of greatness—imaginative skill—by a person who is growing, the teacher will be a great teacher. I am convinced that many of us have the potential to reach a considerable measure of such greatness in teaching if we envision our work properly, if we avoid certain rather simple but deadly traps, and if we over a period of time cultivate the roots of growth toward excellence.

It is of utmost importance that the modern college teacher escape the most fatal conception of all those that afflict teachers: namely, that his principal responsibility is to dispense information. No one has stated this point better than that very wise teacher, scientist, and philosopher, Professor Alfred North Whitehead:[11] "Culture is activity of thought, and receptiveness to beauty and humane feeling. Scraps of information have nothing to do with it. A merely well-informed man is the most useless bore on God's earth." Later in the same essay he says:

"In the history of education, the most striking phenomenon is that schools of learning, which at one epoch are alive with a ferment of genius, in a succeeding generation exhibit merely pedantry and routine. The reason is that they are overladen with inert ideas. Education with inert ideas is not only useless: it is above all things, harmful—CORRUPTIO OPTIMI, PESSIMA. Except at rare intervals of intellectual ferment, education in the past has been radically infected with inert ideas."

The point is made again in his famous essay "Universities and Their Functions" in this way:

The universities are schools of education, and schools of research. But the primary reason for their existence is not to be found either in the mere knowledge conveyed to the students or in the mere opportunities for research afforded to the members of the faculty.

Both these functions could be performed at a cheaper rate, apart from these very expensive institutions. Books are cheap, and the system of apprenticeship is well understood. So far as the mere imparting of information is concerned, no university has had any justification for existence since the popularization of printing in the fifteenth century.

We might be astounded to know how much dispensing of dead knowledge is carried on in the name of teaching in colleges and universities.

Perhaps more important than the escape from being a dispenser of dead knowledge is the development by the college teacher of a clear conception of his role. If he is much more than a mere dispenser of knowledge, a sort of live resource book or encyclopedia, what is that more? How can that role be most meaningfully conceived? Many figures could be used, but the most helpful concept I have found is that of a guide or senior partner on a fascinating journey.

The goal of such a journey in higher education is to provide experience from which certain knowledge, attitudes and skills may arise that become the foundation for the wisdom needed in life. Or since, as Plato says, no mortal can hope to be wise but merely a seeker after wisdom, in essence the goal of this journey or experience would be to produce individuals who would be ardent, lifetime seekers after wisdom — in the deepest sense, philosophers.

The teacher proposes to assist the student in the initial stages of a lifelong odyssey, the purpose of which is the discovery and wise use of significant truth. The assumption is not that the teacher has himself been fully over the course and thus has arrived, but rather that in the climate of the institution of higher learning each teacher highly trained in his specialty may be somewhat more mature and learned about this journey into knowledge and wisdom than those who come to study with him. Thus the teacher hopes to help the students, although he knows that the best learning must be genuine learning together.

The Special Functions of the Teacher

As an expert fellow learner and learning guide, the effective college teacher has four very practical and fundamental functions or responsibilities. Let us now examine each of these briefly.

1. The guide on the journey of learning must plan the objectives of the particular segment of the odyssey for which he is responsible. In reality, education reaches from birth to death and encompasses every aspect of life. But formal education is based upon the theory that man can learn significantly from concentrated, planned, and vicarious experience. The formal curriculum is a selected group of experiences presented in such manner that the learner reaps in a brief school period the benefit of hundreds or even thousands of years of man's experience.

In order to make the varied, complex experience of man manageable in a formal learning situation, it must be broken into segments, or what are commonly called subjects. A teacher will be responsible for providing a part of the student's educational experience in such subjects as American History, Shakespeare, or Basic Principles of Health. Such divisions of knowledge are merely attempts, often clumsy and artificial, to stake out a body of experience to be had at a given level and during a set period of time. The artificial dividing of a garment that is actually seamless does not work too well, for the experience is in constant danger of becoming partial and fragmental, consequently inert, unrelated, and meaningless.

The teacher must have the experience and wisdom to plan the objectives of a course and roughly set its limits. These objectives are most meaningful to the teacher and the student when they are framed in terms of desirable outcomes and of the experiences which are likely to produce those outcomes. The first question is, "What do we want this course, or body of experience, to do for the students who participate in it?"

Such objectives will include large over-all skills and attitudes which are the purpose of all higher learning: for example, the ability to express one's thoughts clearly in writing or in speech; an enduring respect for evidence and methods of its evaluation; the inquiring seeking spirit of the continuous learner; integrity in thought and action. These large objectives, which undergird and are an important part of the process of advanced learning, should be conscious and unconscious outcomes of every course.

Then there are the more specific objectives of a particular segment or course of learning. These vary in terms of the nature of the subject and the level at which it is being studied. Included here will be terminology, facts, principles, attitudes and skills necessary to the fullest and most profitable learning. It is of utmost importance to effective teaching that objectives be clear, related to life so as to be meaningful (that is, worth learning), and, above all, limited so that they can be achieved. Vague and limitless objectives are among the chief sources of poor teaching. To have a clear notion of what can be reasonably expected from this journey together is a great boon to both teacher and taught.

Important as the careful planning of desirable objectives in terms of outcomes may be, I believe the planning of objectives in terms of experience is much more fundamental to great teaching at the college level. The teacher strives to provide the experiences which in the light of his knowledge and wisdom are most likely to produce the contemplated outcomes. The principle here is so simple that its basic nature is likely to be missed. Let us suppose a specific outcome set for a course in composition is a given skill in sentence or paragraph structure. The crucial problem is to plan the specific experiences (things to be done by the students) that are likely to create the attitudes and skills necessary to clear sentence structure.

Or suppose a goal or an objective is an understanding of and appreciation for the dramas of William Shakespeare. What activities on the part of the teacher and the students will most effectively achieve this goal? Or stated in another way, what is the best kind of experience with the plays of Shakespeare?

Perhaps a different kind of example will help to make this point clearer. Let us suppose we wanted a group of students to learn certain things about ancient Greek civilization and as a learning experience we had the opportunity to go with these students on a two months' tour of the Greek lands. Immediately we would be faced with numerous questions: How much and what type of background reading would be most helpful? Where would the journey start, what places would it take in, and where would it end? How much formal writing and recording would be most profitable? When and what type of formal and informal discussion would be provided? How could the journey be intense enough to bring about depth and breadth of learning and yet avoid the clutter and crowdedness which are the prime enemies of the best experiences? How much of the most revealing things in the Greek environment (color, light, spirit) should the learning guide point out and how much should he let the learner see for himself? Obviously these are only a few of the many questions an experienced learning guide would wish to consider both before the journey and during its progress.

Planning is important, but it is well also to remember that any significant journey is a living adventure that unfolds and changes as it progresses. Although the skillful teacher has a general plan of the experiences this particular journey will include, he is always looking for different or additional ones that will do the job better.

One final word about this vital task. The teacher can be sure that every student who has a vivid experience will learn. The nature of man is such that if he is not pathological in some significant way he will learn when he interacts with ideas or objects. He learns from *his* experience (his interaction) and not from the experience of his would-be teacher, but he will learn if he has experience. Thus the great teacher's chief concern is to plan varied and rich experiences for his students, for he knows that out of these experiences learning will arise. The learning will not always be the specific outcomes planned or those measured by formal tests, but often if the activity is alive, imaginative, and varied, the learning which occurs will be more important than that planned. Such must be the faith of the teacher in the human mind.

The first task of the effective teacher then is to plan the objectives of the course or journey in terms of (a) desired outcomes and (b) experiences from which learning will likely arise.

2. The second responsibility of the college teacher is to guide the students so that they will secure economically and effectively the experiences in breadth and depth that will cause them to achieve the desired objectives in terms of their interests, maturity levels, and abilities. However well-planned a journey may be, it will little profit the traveler unless it is taken. A college class may have clear, meaningful, and even appealing objectives carefully formulated by the instructor and still not be an effective class; the problem is to get the students to participate in achieving the objectives.

A teacher falls easily into the error of believing that a map well made and clearly presented means a road meaningfully traveled, or, worse, of believing that if the teacher understands and travels the road, it follows that the students have done so. As described before, the types of experiences that give promise of producing learning have been decided upon; now the central job is to get the students to have the experiences — to engage in the activities, to take the journey.

Nothing mysterious or vague is implied by the term experience. I mean essentially the active engagement in reading, writing, discussion, practice, field work, thought, research, questioning—the activities that the teacher as a trained and experienced guide believes will bring learning.

Here the teacher is faced with the abiding and complex problem of motivation. It is remarkable how much and how rapidly those students learn who want to learn; a similar marvel is the thinness and slowness of learning when the reasons for learning are weak and vague. The teacher who wishes to grow in excellence will make the study of motivation—the means of getting students to participate in the experience that produces learning—a lifetime study. Only one other thing can be said about the problem at this point. The temptation is great to depend largely on the fear of failure or desire for success, expressed by low or high grades. Doubtless, symbols of success have their place and time, but it is well to remember that the best teachers depend little or not at all on these external and largely artificial modes of motivation.

The second phase of the task of teaching is to do everything in one's power to guarantee that the students get the experience upon which learning depends.

3. The third task is closely related to the second, but goes beyond it, and comes, in my judgment, near the heart of effective teaching. It is here that the difference between adequate teaching and great teaching is revealed. I refer to the enlightenment and enrichment of the learning experiences by varied and imaginative stimulation at the level of what Professor Whitehead terms romance, precision, and generalization.[11]

This phase of the teaching process determines the quality of the experience, and hence the quality and depth of learning. We all know that a journey can be an exciting adventure or it can be merely a dull trip, even though geographically the same ground is covered in both cases. The imaginative, creative teacher finds a variety of ways by which the learning is given life, meaning, high interest.

I doubt if any practical suggestions will help much in this phase of teaching. Every aspect of the personality and character of the teacher as a distinct person influences this art of teaching —the style of the individual teacher that really does the job. The great teacher may be humorous or serious; he may encourage or scold; his voice may be resonant and pleasing or squeaky and offensive; he may be warm or relatively distant; he may be an effective speaker or hesitant and stumbling; he may be an immaculate and tasty dresser who makes the coeds sigh or as unkempt and monotonous in dress as Socrates; he may be reputed as hard or soft. In fact, his style may seem to be a combination of contradictions, but the key is that by one means or another the learning experience is brought to life and given meaning.

Some have felt that the key is enthusiasm as seen in William Rainey Harper as he engaged college girls in the study of Hebrew, or in Louis Agassiz as he made the technical study of fish an intriguing adventure either for a graduate student or an unlearned audience on the waterfront. Others have sought the essence of this greatness in imagination as exemplified in William James. It seems that in all of these teachers and others who have given special life to the experience of learning, there was an elemental quality which enabled them to escape pedantry, secondhandedness, and overabstraction, and to achieve a special directness or firsthandedness in dealing with both people and things that gave freshness and life to their own experience and to all they touched.

Perhaps there is a certain mystery about all this as there is about all art in action. The point is that by a variety of means arising out of the very essence of the teacher's personality, the odyssey—the experience—is given life and meaning: then great teaching is done and great learning goes on.

4. The modern teacher has a fourth responsibility at which he must be skilled. He must be able to evaluate the effectiveness of the learning journey. Constantly before his mind are the questions: Is the desired learning taking place? Are the teacher and the learner (indeed they are both learners) getting the amount and type of experience from which learning can arise? Does this experience have imaginative quality—is it alive? In short, he is continuously evaluating the teaching-learning process against the

standard of constantly developing objectives. If the teacher lacks the desire to evaluate or lacks skill, the whole process tends to crystallize or deteriorate.

Hence the teacher who wishes to grow in excellence should understand the extreme significance of this phase of his work. As a rule, in the practical workaday world, teaching will be no better than the teacher's philosophy and technique of testing and evaluating. This principle has both a positive and a negative side.

A constructive, wholesome philosophy and skillful techniques of evaluation make a great contribution in guiding both teacher and student to more effective learning. Such evaluation well done helps to establish the all-important spirit of partnership in both planning and carrying out the learning endeavor. In a purpose-directed effort no questions are more meaningful than, What progress are we making toward our goals? Where are we doing best and where do we seem to be falling short and why? What can we do to improve?

It should be noted that the positive quality of the evaluation process arises from the basic spirit in which it is done. Evaluation in this spirit is a mutual, friendly concern about progress toward mutually accepted meaningful goals. There is thus a minimum of the punitive and smugly judgmental in it. Yet the standards may be as high as vision and ability will permit. Mutual respect and partnership in work do not imply low standards. Indeed, are not the highest standards in life those set by purpose, loyalty, honor and love?

One of the most prevalent and potent obstacles to effective teaching is the negative aspect of testing or evaluation. This spectre rises to spoil nearly all learning from the third or fourth grade on. The evaluation of learning becomes by various means separated from the learning process as a whole. Instead of being a means of guiding and helping learning, it becomes a punitive instrument associated with the teacher. The student thus is set over against the teacher, and a fatal game is inaugurated that usually continues throughout the whole formal learning period, to the conferring of the last degree.

From this noxious root a multitude of poisonous plants grow that come very near transforming what should be the pleasant garden of learning into a poison-laden wilderness. The young mind is ingenious and tries to turn the whole process into a game —a sort of undeclared war—in which the students are pitted against the institution and its teachers. With the growing emphasis on grades as the final symbol of achievement the struggle becomes a life and death matter.

Only a few of the practical evil effects of bad testing are mentioned here. The thoughtful teacher can multiply the list almost indefinitely. Most serious of all, the climate of learning or the optimum learning situation is destroyed or seriously harmed by bad testing. A spirit of antagonism and fear between the guide and his fellow travelers does not make for the most profitable journey.

A second effect is a growing artificial and even negative attitude toward learning. A great old teacher of mine, Professor Henry C. Morrison of the University of Chicago, called it "the lesson-learning attitude." As this attitude grows, the student comes to value satisfying the tester (and this can be in trying to prepare for any test, good or bad) above the actual learning. Thus, the externally-controlled symbol comes to dominate the learner's concern. Often he will go to any means, including gross cheating or harming his friend or neighbor, to secure the desired symbol (grade).

Another serious effect of bad testing is its destructive influence on the teacher. Very frequently the teacher who would like to be a great learning guide, highly trained and widely experienced, eager to open up the intriguing vistas of learning, wakes up to find himself cast in the role of an arbitrary, unfair, often mean-spirited taskmaster. Thus, the image of the teacher is besmirched and distorted and the effectiveness of his work undermined.

Further emphasis on the significance of evaluation is not needed here. Perhaps the point is clear that one of the major responsibilities of the teacher is skillful, constructive evaluation of the learning process, both its ends and means.

Thus we see that excellence in teachers requires inspired or growing skill in four great processes: planning of objectives in terms of outcomes and experiences; assisting the students to get the experience that will produce learning; enriching and enlightening the learning experience to give it life and meaning, and evaluating the learning so as to contribute to the optimum climate or condition of learning.

I believe the essences of the optimum learning situation are high enthusiasm for the adventure of learning and mutual respect among learners—teacher and taught. Without the spirit of inquiry and discovery, learning will be slow, shallow, narrow, and unpleasant. One will learn little from a guide he does not respect. It is equally true that for the best results the guide must respect the potential and goals of those whom he would influence. Indeed, at best, it seems there is an element of identification and love in the most creative teacher-learner relationship. The interested teacher should examine Gardner Murphy's thoughtful little book, *Freeing Intelligence Through Teaching.*[12]

Growth toward Excellence in College Teaching: Background Factors

Earl V. Pullias

This chapter is based on the assumption that the college teacher understands something of the meaning of higher education and its vital role in the life of a free society, and has at least an elementary grasp of the nature of the work of the modern teacher. Such a teacher feels the power and challenge of his profession and longs to grow toward the highest level of excellence or greatness his abilities and circumstances of life will allow. For him, these informal tentative suggestions about college teaching and some of the major conditions for the optimum climate of learning may be helpful. The thoughtful teacher will recognize that in the case of each principle only the barest sketch or hint is given here. Detail, full analysis of implications, needed qualifications, modes of practical application are left for the inquiring fellow teacher to fill in.

There is no inclination to pontificate or lay down the word about teaching and learning at the college level. Whatever else thirty years or so studying and practicing college teaching may do for and to the reasonably sensitive and sincere person, at least it makes him humble in the presence of the problems—keenly aware of how little he knows and how little is known about the vital subject of teaching and learning. These ideas are offered, then, in the hope of stimulating further thought and in the spirit of a continuous search for helpful insights.

The Influence of the Institution as a Whole

The college or university as a living community of learners develops "a spirit of place" which is the most powerful single factor in the process of higher education. Teachers are important, students are crucial, libraries and laboratories are necessary. But the institution as a whole, dedicated to and engaged in the process of the higher learning, is greater than and different from any single part that makes it up.

No one has yet or perhaps ever will be able to define or fully describe the "spirit of place" that makes an institution of higher learning. One gets a glimpse of its essence by reading a book like Samuel Eliot Morison's *Three Centuries of Harvard;*[1] or perhaps a more living and meaningful grasp from the thirty-nine essays that make up *A College in a Yard.*[2] Many teachers have found Ordway Tead's *Climate of Learning*[3] the most helpful brief statement on the subject. A research-centered study such as the recently published *Pioneer: A History of the Johns Hopkins University,*[4] by Hugh Hawkins, presents the matter from another angle. The accounts of the development of institutions of higher learning and their work and influence are numerous. They vary enormously in literary quality and depth of insight, but nearly all of them convey the feeling that these institutions, large and small, old and young, famous and unknown, have a quality as institutions which has a profound influence on all who participate in their processes.

Although no method has been developed by which this quality can be measured and placed on a scale, doubtless colleges and universities vary greatly in the spirit of place or learning atmosphere which is so potent in producing the optimum learning climate. Age and traditions are probably important factors, although they do not seem to be absolutely necessary. Under the leadership of William Rainey Harper, Chicago became a great place of learning within a single generation. Buildings certainly are important, but one can recall few institutions that had greater power than the London School of Economics at the height of its influence; yet its buildings were not impressive. People are certainly important, but this factor too is elusive.

It is not our purpose here to make a full analysis of the factors that seem to contribute to the spirit of place that makes a great institution, as interesting and profitable as such an analysis might be. It is enough at this point that teachers be aware of the significance of the intellectual, sociological, spiritual, and physical *gestalt* in which their work goes on. Then perhaps they may come to have a greater appreciation for and responsibility to the integrity of their institutions as living organisms.

Under the best conditions all who are a part of the institution and especially the senior members of the community, the faculty, strive to create the atmosphere in which the process of higher learning can flourish: a tolerant, kindly, persistent, exciting, exacting search for truth and for its most effective incarnation into the varied processes of life. To become a part of such a living community of learners, as teacher and student, is to take part in the fullest realization of one's potential.

No college teacher will achieve his optimum power who is not strengthened, supported, and inspired by an awareness of and perhaps a humble pride in his institution as a whole. At the same time, a warning should be sounded that the spirit of place, the atmosphere of learning, like the morale of a good home or the spiritual power of a great church, is best when it exists inconspicuously, and even is largely unconscious, working like old Lao-Tzu's Tao.[5]

The fact that the institution as a whole is a potent educational influence has many implications. The present idea of the college or university has developed over a period of about a thousand years in Western civilization. Its forms must be constantly changed to meet the needs of changing society, but care should be taken that in tinkering with its processes its essences are not destroyed. No one can be sure what these essences are, but efforts based upon economy or other expediencies to crowd the educative process by reducing its duration, to depersonalize the learning situation by limiting markedly the interaction among teachers and students should be examined with great caution before they are applied widely.

If the institution as such educates, then it is important that the institution retain and cultivate its unique educative qualities and that teachers and students have the opportunity of being en-meshed in the central life of the living organism.

An Understanding of the Nature and Tradition
of the Higher Learning

The college teacher is a member of one of the oldest and most influential of the professions. His calling carries with it high privileges and heavy responsibilities. He is much more likely to achieve excellence in his work if he understands and appreciates the distinctive nature of the higher learning of which he is a part and the relation it holds to a developing society.

An attempt was made to state briefly the essence of the nature and purpose of higher education in Chapter 1. I should like to recommend strongly that college teachers make a special effort to acquaint themselves with the history of colleges and universities as they have developed in Western civilization. A very elemen-tary knowledge of the European background will enable the teacher to follow with keen interest the major developments of higher education in the United States. A relatively full knowl-edge of the developments in America will contribute greatly to the teacher's effectiveness.

A modern college faculty member is expected to assume much responsibility for almost every phase of the work of the institu-tion where he serves. The faculty members who achieve tenure, and of course many of them do, become a permanent aspect of the college. Student generations come and go, administrative officers change, but the tenure faculty are the institution in con-tinuity. Through committee work and in various advisory rela-tions they make the decisions that are vital to the welfare, prog-ress, and quality of their college or university.

The faculty member will make wiser and more mature deci-sions if he is well informed about the background and history of the problems. For example, colleges and universities in the United States have wrestled with the following problems over the past 300 years: (1) curriculum content and organization; (2) the nature and purpose of higher learning; (3) graduation requirements; (4) faculty rights and privileges; (5) optimum student-faculty relationships; (6) board-administration-faculty relationships; (7) faculty tenure and retirement; (8) academic freedom and its relation to higher learning; (9) town and gown relations; (10) promotion; (11) teaching and research; (12) evaluation of teaching; (13) admissions; (14) student behavior, and so on.

I am aware that the highly specialized teacher is busy with his specialization and likely will not wish to pursue at length the study of higher education. Advanced technical knowledge in this area is not necessary to effectiveness as a college teacher, but ignorance of the basic facts of one's profession is a serious obstacle to growth toward excellence. A teacher called upon to discuss and reach decisions about such problems as those listed in the foregoing paragraph will not only be more efficient, reasonable, and tolerant in his decisions but will respect himself more and be a happier professional worker if his discussions and decisions are based upon some grasp of what is known about the problems.

Fortunately a very fine professional literature is developing in the area of higher education. The average teacher cannot keep abreast with all this research and writing; yet I believe he will find his profession much more meaningful if he reads some of the best books and articles that appear each year. An acquaintance with some of these writings enables the teacher to put his own classroom and campus work within the meaning-giving framework and perspective of the thought and action of the profession as a whole. Without such perspective it is easy, almost inevitable, for the teacher to become overspecialized, narrow, isolated, and poorly related to students, colleagues, and life.

Many alert faculties, in addition to their own personal professional libraries which naturally would be limited, are developing a professional reading shelf in the faculty lounge or some other convenient place. Fifty to a hundred basic items make a good foundational shelf, and then the addition of ten to fifteen new books a year will keep the collection growing and alive. If reading and discussion groups are organized, a faculty may develop intense interest in the problems of higher education, and without too much effort may keep themselves informed on the best current thought about their profession. This writing and research is done largely by practicing college teachers. Perhaps in the future more and more thoughtful college teachers will enter this great exchange of ideas on higher education through writing. Teachers interested in developing a reading shelf will find more detailed suggestions, including a tentative list of books, in "A Professional Reading Shelf for College Faculties."[6]

Expertness in an Area of Man's Experience

The college teacher should have excellent training in the area of his special responsibility. In view of the very rapid growth in college enrollment there is almost certain to be a growing shortage of teachers who have completed the work for a doctorate in the area of their specialization. The facts seem to indicate that if the colleges are staffed, as they must be, there will be a smaller proportion of college teachers who hold the doctorate ten years from now than have that level of training at present. Roughly 40 per cent of college and university teachers had the doctorate in 1960; a widely publicized estimate suggests that the figure will be as low as 23 per cent by 1970. This estimate is probably low, but no one questions that the problem will be acute.

I am not suggesting that every college teacher can or should have the training represented by the doctorate. Further, I am acquainted with the varied criticisms that have been made of the research doctorate and its adequacy as preparation for college teaching. Whatever the answer to these problems may be, the point is still fundamental that as a foundation for growth toward excellence in college teaching, the teacher needs highly specialized training. He cannot be a great learning guide unless he knows well the area of experience for which he is responsible. Whatever may be said in criticism of the Ph.D. or similar degree as it is now given, in my judgment it is the best available training for college teaching. This degree should be, I believe, the goal of the teacher who wishes to make the most of his profession. If this amount of special study cannot be done, the goal should be as much study beyond the typical Master's work as time, energy, and ability will allow.

The question is frequently asked, "Why is such advanced study important for the undergraduate teacher who will be teaching relatively introductory courses?" The question is not easy to answer for it involves the whole theory of the college experience. If the teacher merely imparted knowledge or taught the elementary techniques and principles, textbook fashion, of an area of study, then perhaps a mastery of the specifics to be taught would suffice. But, as has been mentioned, the responsibility of the college teacher is to teach or guide students in an "imaginative consideration" of an area of man's experience. His leadership will not be respected, the consideration will be thin and narrow, and the stimulation shallow if he has minimum training. Further, the poorly trained teacher tends to lack confidence and, instead of striking out boldly into the deeper and more intriguing areas of his subject, fearfully clings close to the dull shore.

The notion that a teacher who has achieved excellent foundational training (let us say, the doctorate) can then consider himself expert once and for all is a great threat to excellence in college teaching. The college teacher must, above almost all else, be a continuous learner. Perhaps it was never possible, but certainly now the "mastery" of an area of knowledge is a myth. One needs a beginning mastery, a background of depth, of his area of study, but such mastery is only a beginning. The best college teacher is forever learning his area of specialization; if this is not so, he is almost sure to become that horror of horrors so prevalent among us: a dispenser of inert knowledge. And dead knowledge is not only dull and useless; it is harmful to both teacher and student.

As the teacher continues to learn in his area, he must avoid two pitfalls. Overspecialization of interest, knowledge, and skill can produce a limiting narrowness and even a distasteful snobbery. The other danger is a promiscuous spreading of knowledge and interest that tends to breed mediocrity. The teacher who aspires to greatness must continuously strive for the balance between these two extremes. Expertness that rests upon depth of study but which has a life-enhancing breadth is the teacher's goal. Such balance can result only from much and continuous formal and informal study.

It thus may be said that in learning, as in other phases of life, expertness — mastery — greatly enhances the effectiveness of a guide. It is important that such expertness be worn lightly; like the well-dressed person's clothes, it must not be particularly noticeable to him or to others.

Wide Reading and Experience Outside the Teacher's Specialty

The teacher's expertness in his specialty is both a strength and a weakness; a necessary condition for great teaching and a constant threat to its quality. Modern life seems to demand high specialization, and the pressure for increasingly narrow specialization mounts steadily. It is very nearly impossible for any person to keep abreast of the varied research and discussion in even a relatively limited area of study. But this apparently necessary concentration on one phase of knowledge or thought tends to make one's work in his specialty lose its breadth—its relatedness to all other learning—and hence much of its larger meaning and interest. This is the threat in specialization. Yet, as we have discussed elsewhere in this chapter, a high level of mastery of a limited field is prerequisite to excellence in teaching.

How can this dilemma be overcome? I wish to urge the habit of wide reading outside one's field. Unfortunately, significant research on this point is not available, but experience with teachers leads me to conclude that the highly effective college teacher will as a rule be a wide and continuous reader outside his area of professional specialization.

Through constant and planned extension of experience by reading, the teacher enriches and broadens his understanding and appreciation of his specific subject. His store of illustration, fundamental to all effective teaching, is plentiful, varied, and contemporary. Even more important, such reading tends to keep the personality of the teacher flexible and attractive. Alive to the life and thought of the world, he is more likely to keep his teaching alive. All that he brings to his classes is balanced, sobered, and enriched by its having been related in his own mind to other learning.

The reading program will vary in terms of the interests and experiences of particular teachers. One hesitates to give advice on such matters, yet the danger of creeping or even galloping narrowness is so great that perhaps a few suggestions are not amiss. Drifting is so easy that some conscious planning is wise for almost all teachers.

A teacher will profit greatly from reading some of the best of current fiction. The question is, How much? Perhaps the best approach is to peruse regularly the book review sections of at least two good magazines in order to find items that seem to have promise. Personally, I look regularly at *Saturday Review, The Atlantic Monthly,* and the *New York Times Book Review.* Reviews in no sense should take the place of reading the books. There is as much difference between actually reading a good book and reading even the best review as there is between reading about being in love and being in love; or looking at swimming and really swimming. The reviews should be used chiefly to find titles of books that one may wish to read.

Of course fiction is only one aspect of current literature; biography, history, criticism, travel, philosophy all have their value and appeal. Then there are well-written magazines that carry material of great interest and meaning.

When this point about reading outside the professional specialty is made to advanced graduate students, many already teaching in college, they throw up their hands and proclaim they simply cannot afford the time to read. In rushed modern life, of course, time is a serious problem. Yet the teacher who wishes to grow toward excellence cannot afford to neglect his reading any more than he could afford to neglect his diet because he wanted to spend the money on something else. Some things are fundamental and hence have priority; wide reading is one of these for the teacher who would achieve excellence.

Much else could be said about reading but two or three practical suggestions must suffice. Whether reading matter is good or not is somewhat a matter of taste, but there is an enormous difference in both the content and style of written matter. I suggest that since the teacher's time is so limited, he form the habit of reading the best writing he can find. The thought, style, vocabulary of great books will directly enrich the teacher's work and it simply is not true that good books are dull. For example, two excellent pieces of fiction which appeared early in 1962 are keenly interesting, thoughtful, and informative. I refer to Mary Renault's

The Bull From the Sea,[7] and Richard Hughes' *The Fox in the Attic.*[8]

Some teachers may wish to keep an informal notebook on reading outside their specialty. I have kept such a notebook for about twenty years, usually writing a brief informal impression of the book when it is completed. These notes are interesting to re-examine from time to time and are a valuable source of ideas.

Many teachers have found it stimulating to buy a good book now and then and after it is read lend it to friends. If a special place is provided on the back flyleaf for a sentence reaction, many friends will be pleased to respond. Thus a book may have the date of reading and the reactions of five or six friends. In this way, one's own interest is enhanced, interchange of thought is promoted, and reading is increased. Of course, eventually the book may disappear, but that really doesn't matter.

Probably college teachers will have already developed or will think of many other devices that will keep the habit of wide reading alive and growing. I repeat, here perhaps more than anywhere else lies the key to staying alive as a teacher.

4

Growth toward Excellence in College Teaching: Personal Factors

Earl V. Pullias

The Understanding of Modern Youth

There is a certain natural antagonism between generations—between youth and age. In the process of life the old are replaced by the young. A partial awareness of this inevitable cycle creates an underlying groundwork of tension that influences all human relations. However great the love and respect may be between father and son, always present and affecting the relation is the fact that it is the destiny of the son to replace the father, and the fate of the father to decline and be replaced. Neither does the oft romanticized relation between mother and daughter escape this tension. In general, people seldom face these facts squarely. More often they pretend that all is well between age and youth; understanding deteriorates, distance between them increases, and latent hostility and antagonism boil to the surface in various forms of behavior. An insightful analysis of this complex problem can be found in Professor Bruno Bettelheim's article, "The Problem of Generations."[1]

The college teacher, in the main, works with late youth and early adulthood. Growth in excellence as a teacher is thus greatly dependent upon a living, growing knowledge of youth in all its strange complexity. It is equally important that the teacher understand the psychology of growing older, of seeing the physiological, psychological, and sociological gap between him and his students grow wider each year. One old teacher who has been very skillful in teaching remarked to me, "I have come to feel myself a stranger among my students."

There is no simple solution to this problem for it roots in the very nature of the cycle of life, but there are two approaches that will help the thoughtful teacher to bridge the ever-widening gap between youth and age. One is a continuous study by every means possible of the nature of the problems of youth, in an attempt to develop a sympathetic understanding of behavior of youth and its probable causes. The other is a study of age and the aging process with special emphasis upon the major factors involved in the relations between age and youth. This second approach is a lifelong study in self-understanding.

Fortunately, there is a growing body of research on the modern college student: his attitudes, interests, and special problems. Much of this work has been briefly summarized in a pamphlet, *They Come for the Best of Reasons*,[2] by W. Max Wise. It seems that a teacher tends to stereotype and crystallize his conceptions about youth at some particular time in his professional career. After that the notions stubbornly resist change. For example, doubtless thousands of college teachers formed the picture of "Joe College" years ago and continue basically to view each new generation of college students in this way. Such research as we have seems to indicate clearly that Joe College with his coonskin coat, his aggressively nonchalant attitudes, and his respect for the gentleman's "C" has long since ceased to be even vaguely typical. Probably he never was actually typical, but many students and faculty believed or pretended to believe that he was.

And what do recent studies suggest the college student is like? The picture is confused, as it must be, but in general he is portrayed as fearfully earnest, hardworking almost to a fault, predominantly conscious of security, greatly concerned about social, religious, and philosophic problems, and extremely grade conscious. A thorough and varied discussion of the modern college student can be found in Nevitt Sanford's recent book, *The American College*.[3] In my judgment, this portrait, although having some basis in fact, is also a caricature just as Joe College was a caricature.

Perhaps the important point for the teacher is that youth, like all other things, is forever changing. Just when one is ready to smugly generalize about the youth of one generation, a new and somewhat different generation is already arising. This does not mean that studies and neat conclusions about the nature of youth are worthless, but that the study must be continuous, and that all generalizations must be taken with a generous pinch of salt. Else the teacher may find himself working, as is the tendency of a pedant, in terms of abstractions that no longer have close and meaningful relation to reality.

The growing teacher's understanding of young people should rest upon a knowledge of the best literature on the subject, but should not stay there. No formal knowledge can do the work of direct experience. The teacher is constantly in a psychological laboratory. If he is sensitive and thoughtful, every contact he has with youth can be a source of deeper understanding. I would urge that should the picture of youth as found in books not coincide with the picture built up from direct study, then the latter should have the greater weight. Youth as they are, as observed in day-to-day relations, rarely fit any generalized image. In short, the wise teacher strives to keep his views of youth flexible, altering former conclusions by constant observation.

In addition to the use of research, theoretical writing, and sensitive sympathetic direct observation, there is another approach to the understanding of youth that is less direct but can be very profitable. With some effort most teachers can recall something of their own youth. A survey of one's own youth, if one has the courage to make it frankly and honestly, is a great assistance in understanding all youth. What were some of our feelings, attitudes, ambitions, fears, hopes, hostilities during the period of our youth? What motivations brought us to college? And would we dare review some of our behavior?

This approach to the deeper understanding of youth has great possibilities, but it is difficult and painful to use. Every year the teacher is one year farther from his own youth and its problems. As a natural defense, the memories that remain are romanticized and blurred. Gradually by this process the person loses contact with his own youth, thus with a chief source of understanding the interests, needs, and problems of the young. Only a very thoughtful person can recall the poignant pain that accompanies being embarrassed before one's peers, of not having proper dress for an occasion, of being ignored by one whose fa-

vor is greatly desired, of holding in check overwhelming physical
and psychological needs. The adult finds it almost impossible to
face these memories. If they are available to him in some vivid-
ness, he tends to rationalize or discount them by thinking it would
be different were he young again.

It is useful to face a paradox at this point. Although it is true
that youth is constantly changing, each generation differing from
another, it is equally true that there are basic ways in which the
youth of all generations are alike. The most durable and useful
understanding must rest upon a grasp of the essences which grow
out of the very nature of man. My relatively long experience in
dealing with a wide variety of college youth leads me to conclude that the overt differences between generations of youth are
relatively surface in nature. This overt behavior usually reflects
current modes of thought, language, and social behavior and the
surface customs of family and locality.

Beneath all this there is a deeper part of youth which changes
little from generation to generation or even from culture to culture. Often these profound qualities are hidden from others, especially those of an older generation. Sincerity and mutual respect in many cases can enable both youth and adult to go beneath the defensive and deceptive surface or façade, and then
there can be a creative, healing, and growth-producing meeting
of deeper, more genuine selves.

In such relations, which are delicate and perhaps even dangerous, the surface differences and resulting antagonisms disappear
and age and youth may meet, for a little while at least, in a realm
that is timeless. At this depth artificial barriers dissolve and men
are men whatever their age, their culture, their time of sojourn
on this planet. Here concerns, interests, fears, needs, longings express essences and rest upon realities. Such understanding so
longed for by all mortals and so rarely achieved is the goal of
every teacher who aspires to excellence in his art. Without at
least some understanding at the depth that approaches universals,
much of the teacher's work bears the destructive burden of pretense, a wasteful sparring with youth.

Only a word can be said about the teacher's growth in self-
understanding as a means to a better relation with youth. The
adventure of development from youth to old age—in the case of
the teacher, to retirement—has many hazards. If these are not

well understood by the maturing and aging person, they may become serious obstacles to good relations between the young and the more mature. There is a tendency for all teachers to become oracular. They sometimes feel they have the final authoritative word and may resent its being questioned by brash youth. Often fear and defensiveness accompany the loss of one's powers. Energy is less, bodily attractiveness decreases, imagination is less vivid. The maturing person who lacks wisdom and self-understanding may unconsciously resent youth in whom attractive physical and mental qualities are so apparent.

Life is a journey by stages from birth to death. In most people there seems to be a deep need to halt the process at some particular point, and to resent the forces of youth and fate that say there can be no stopping. Each stage has its strengths and great joys. The wise teacher accepts this process of maturing and growing old in a spirit of adventure. At best he finds joy in the rising strength and unfolding powers of the young who are seen as partners and fellow workers rather than antagonists.

Perhaps the most important aspect of a teacher's understanding of youth is a respect for and keen interest in the potential in human nature. All that we have been able to learn from psychological research and general observation leads to the conclusion that the abilities of man are very great and almost infinitely varied. The teacher who would grow in greatness must respect the material with which he works—the complex human body, mind, and spirit working as personality. His feeling for the potential and sacredness of his material is not unlike that of the master workman using wood, or stone, or color, or words for his medium. A teacher who has not achieved this respect and appreciation for the human material with which he works, or who has allowed the hammer blows of practical life to make him cynical about people, can hardly hope to rise toward excellence in the art of teaching.

The Health of the Teacher

Health broadly conceived is the most urgent problem of modern times. The human personality is a complex unity of body, mind, and spirit. We will not pause here to try to limit or define each of these aspects of the whole self. It will suffice for our purposes to think of body, mind, and spirit as they are conceived in literature or in ordinary life. In the functioning individual these three aspects of the person are in such intricate relation that it is very nearly impossible to separate them. Each has subtle and profound influence upon the other. It would be regrettable if some teacher, perhaps misguided by a special emphasis or interest, should be offended by the simple terms "body," "mind," "spirit," and thus feel constrained to deny the realities which they represent. The body, mind, and spirit of man seem to exist in quite meaningful manifestations, however men may argue over terminology.

Perhaps no people in the history of the world have so nearly achieved the optimum balanced unity as the ancient Greeks. Hence no people have come so near to demonstrating the full potential of man. Few people have described more accurately and inspiringly this height of health to which men can rise than the English historian C. M. Bowra in *The Greek Experience*.[4]

The important point here is that the human personality varies enormously in the effectiveness of its functioning. Health is the term used to describe the degree of this effectiveness. Extremes are easy to observe and classify: the very well and the seriously sick. Most people in modern life are neither seriously ill nor vibrantly healthy. Perhaps viewed in terms of what could be, it may be said that modern man is predominantly ill. He rarely functions in any area of his life up to or even near his full potential.

Whole, well-integrated, at its best, the human personality as a unit and functioning in each of its three large aspects of body, mind, and spirit is a magnificent instrument for the living of life. My hypothesis is that, functioning reasonably well and hence guided by the truth and inspiration available to it, the human personality is adequate to all the problems which face it now and will face it in the future. But sick, tired, ill-used, and self-abused man is only part man; his energies are small, his perceptions are dull and distorted, and his motivations are perverted by fear and hatred. Thus he behaves foolishly, hurting himself and others.

Yet the potential is still there and, apparently, largely unimpaired. All of the foolish actions of the past have not destroyed or, it seems, seriously threatened the possibilities of man. Essentially their full realization awaits a step forward in civilization when the basic conditions of life are designed to protect, strengthen, and enrich the health of man.

But we are teachers now in this present stage of man. To grow toward excellence as persons and teachers, we must be reasonably well in a world that is not very well, and this applies to body, to mind, and to spirit.

The teacher's personality (in the broad sense in which the term is used here) is the instrument with which he works. The effective learning guide uses every aspect of the self to assist the fellow travelers to make the journey most profitable. A high level of bodily energy, freedom and clarity in thought, and unity and peace of soul contribute mightily to the art of teaching.

Obviously a full analysis of the health of the teacher cannot be undertaken in this volume. It is enough at this point to urge the crucial importance of health and to suggest a few simple principles that may help the working teacher to protect his health. A few suggestions that other teachers have found helpful follow.

1. Strive to learn the limits of your personality. A person is not unlike a bridge in the sense that there is a limit to the weight it can bear. Most students of this subject agree that each personality has a breaking point—a point beyond which, if the pressure continues, the personality in some phase of itself will begin to develop symptoms which are often merely inappropriate and desperate defenses against unbearable demands. The problem here is for the teacher to learn to reduce demands well before the breaking point is reached. In health, especially in mental health but perhaps in all phases, there is a "point of no return" beyond which there may be great suffering, and a restoration of health may require prolonged professional care.

2. Practice regular and systematic withdrawal and renewal. The wise teacher develops his "great good place" (to use the phrase of Henry James)[5] to which he goes bodily and psychologically to recreate and restore himself. Perhaps the "place" is not so important *as a place*, but rather as the atmosphere which renews—which takes one out of himself if only for a short period, which gives the glorious feeling of freedom from demand, which is a real moment of respite between that which has been completed and that which has not yet begun. Each individual must find his own most helpful means of withdrawal and renewal; and the good means are as varied as life.

I believe that modern individuals, especially those in cities, need regular and close contact with nature. Few things are more healing and refreshing than interaction with forest, land, sea, desert, stream, or the open sky. Also, there are music, the quiet walk, reading, sports, the theater, meditation, unrestrained talk with friends, worship, and many other activities. Every person and especially every teacher has the need for renewal; each is urged not to delay finding his great good place.

3. Develop a few mental and spiritual intimates. In a sense, as the English poet Donne said, "No man is an island. . ." but in another sense, equally deep, every person as an individual is alone, or at least often feels alone which is not very different. Mounting evidence seems to indicate that modern technology which in many ways has brought men closer together in physical proximity, crowding them in cities and on freeways and on battlefields, has in reality made satisfying nearness more difficult among human beings and between people and nature. Therefore, a characteristic of modern persons is loneliness with an undertone of anxiety. The teacher who wishes to bring his best to his art—who, in a word, hopes to be well—must find constructive ways of overcoming this aloneness.

Almost no one can deal with the demands of human life alone. There is unbelievable strength in partnership. An ancient adage expresses this truth: Joys shared are multiplied; troubles shared are divided. In essence, it is a great help to health to be able to share the experiences of life in mutual respect and full confidence. But the relationship must be right, or it will add to the burden. Such "rightness" cannot be expected with many people, hence the suggestion to seek a few intimates. Few relationships are of such quality as to permit uninhibited sharing of triumphs and joys, of frustrations and sorrows. Yet it is the uninhibited expression of these feelings that is vital to the soothing healing of wounds and the satisfying process of growth. Such release and positive expression of concerns, strangely enough, contribute to the well-being of all three large phases of personality: body, mind, and spirit.

Unfortunately, the conditions and processes of work of nearly all teachers are fraught with friction and tension. Such tension tends to accompany the maturing process of young people, particularly in highly civilized societies, and is an inevitable part of the conditions of the teacher's work. This situation cannot and should not be avoided. The typical lack of warmth and understanding among the adults in a college or university environment is a special hazard to the teachers' health and is a general evil that can be eliminated. An atmosphere of jealousy, suspicion, anxious climbing, and fear (expressed in a tendency to play safe in word and action) adds greatly to the natural demands of hard work.

An atmosphere of good will, mutual trust, and common joy in achievement would contribute immeasurably to the teacher's health and effectiveness, but such conditions are rare in the framework of modern life. Thus the wise teacher attempts to develop a few intimates with whom he overcomes the gnawing loneliness so common, especially in current professional life.

Three simple suggestions about the maintenance of health have been given. There is a fine literature on all phases of this subject. Although it would not be good for the teacher to become morbidly concerned about health, surely no subject is more important to the teacher's effectiveness. Probably the zest for life which contributes much to teaching skill is dependent in large measure upon good health.

The Quality of Life or Imagination

He who would be effective in teaching must cultivate the quality of life in his work. The central characteristic of life, in this sense, is imagination. A great enemy of excellence in teaching is pedantry—the ardent and pious dealing in dead knowledge. As mentioned previously, Professor Whitehead observes that the pedant (the person encyclopedically informed in dead knowledge) is the most useless bore on earth; and that knowledge is like fish—it does not keep well; at best it must be fresh from the sea. And by the sea here he means the experience of both the teacher and the student to which the learning must be meaningfully related.

But evidently much of formal learning must come from vicarious experience and hence cannot be closely and meaningfully related to actual life. This gap can be bridged by imagination guided by the teacher and participated in by younger learners.

The effective teacher by apt and imaginative illustrations puts the thing to be learned—whether fact or principle—into new perspective. Through this process both teacher and student constantly discover new and more meaningful relationships and the whole process of learning and teaching is enlightened and enlivened. In this situation, perception, memory, insight—indeed all of the qualities of mind—touched with life lose their wonted sluggishness, and surprise teacher and taught with their bright creativeness. Curiosity and joy in discovery recover some of the freshness of childhood, so evident and pleasing to witness before the young mind takes its fateful journey into the long night of overabstraction and pedantry. Most important for learning, interest and meaning release energy which flows freely into ardent effort.

What has just been said is somewhat theoretical, and there is a danger that its practical implications may escape the working teacher. If imagination is a key to growth toward excellence in teaching, what are some of the practical evidences of this quality?

1. The imaginative teacher must have sufficient mastery of his area of teaching and its relation to other aspects of life to produce confidence and to permit maneuverability or flexibility in ideas and action. The fearful, insecure individual hugs the shore of his subject and can never quite allow himself or others the risky luxury of fresh combinations of ideas. Fear and inadequacy are bulwarks of deadening pedantry.

2. The imaginative teacher must conceive his major function as a teacher correctly. He must in some way escape the age-old conception of himself as a taskmaster and a disher-out of stored (and hence likely decaying) knowledge, and conceive himself as a guide who stimulates and enlivens the learning climate. He must learn to remember that what a teacher covers, does, demands, says is of no importance except as it causes or enables the student to learn.

3. The imaginative teacher must be sufficiently well mentally (this is a matter of degree of course) to be reasonably free. This point is related to mastery of one's area or field of study, but is different. One may have a good knowledge of his teaching area, but be so full of harmful attitudes about himself and others that he cannot throw knowledge and principles into new and creative combinations, nor can he face new applications without great pain.

4. The imaginative teacher has a keen awareness of the human potential with which he works. He tends to have faith in what it can do and be when awakened to growth; and that faith is often the starting point and beginning step in the realization of that which is possible. Here I am reminded of a sentence spoken of the teacher, Robert Frost, by his lifelong friend, Sidney Cox, in that excellent little volume, A *Swinger of Birches*:

And he didn't see anything that wasn't there; he was too genuine and clear-seeing to be fooled. But his seeing what was there made it swell like a sun-stirred seed.[6]

These are merely hints about the nature of teaching which is alive and life-producing as contrasted to that which is dead and stifles the breath of the living mind. The teacher longing to grow toward excellence will cultivate the roots of life in all his thought and activity.

Growth as a Person

What the individual is as a person has a profound influence on his effectiveness as a teacher. Personality and character are the instruments by which all teaching is done. Teaching is in a sense the mediation of experience, or of the result of experience, to those who are learning. The self of the teacher is a sort of prism which breaks up the "light" that is being considered and casts it into fresh relations, and hence gives it varying color. As previously noted, imagination and freedom of mind (which may be the same thing) are vital to this process.

All that the person knows and is learning; all that he is and is becoming—the vitality and well-being of his body, the freedom and flexibility of his mind, the basic concerns and quality of his spirit—are important to his teaching skill. It may be that a half-sick, low-energy, irritable person can be an acceptable teacher and stay on the job a long time, but he will not likely be an effective teacher. Effective teaching requires an abundant supply of energy. A poorly-informed, narrowly-trained subject matter specialist whose mind hovers tenaciously around a few preconceptions and who has respect only for abilities much like his own can be an average, or in some senses, a better than average teacher, but he will not be a great teacher. The arrogant, cynical, selfishly climbing person who disdains concern for truth, beauty, goodness, and love as sentimentality can and does hold classes in a thousand college and university classrooms, but I am confident that such an attitude is a great handicap to growth toward excellence in teaching.

All of this is to say that the most fundamental principle of all we have considered about excellence in teaching is that if the teacher would effectively fulfill his role as a teacher, he must constantly grow in greatness as a person. In deepest essence, a teacher can be no greater as a teacher than he is as a person. The aphorism "What you are speaks so loud I cannot hear what you say" is no more applicable anywhere in life than in teaching.

There are dangers here against which warning should be given. There is no one set of specific personality traits that is best for teaching. What often would seem to be insurmountable handicaps can be overcome, or used as a means to effective teaching. For example, an attractive bodily appearance would seem to be a great asset, but people who are not at all attractive physically can be great teachers. Who has not had a teacher whose negative appearance is forgotten or even loved and revered when the whole self is revealed in action and thought? Who has not been impressed by attractive appearance and apparent charm upon first meeting a teacher to find the surface glitter fade or become distorted as the emptiness behind the facade is revealed?

There is room for a wide variety of personal styles in teaching. In truth, superficial qualities that are quickly evident are very deceptive, both negative and positive ones. So the wise teacher does not give undue weight to surface traits, especially those that might seem to be handicaps. Rather he strives to cultivate the roots that sustain genuine, deep personality and character growth so that he may be in process of becoming the best person physically, mentally, and spiritually his innate potential will allow.

I hesitate to mention specific aspects of personality that are vital to excellence in teaching, for like most other significant things in life they cannot be achieved by directly seeking for them. They arise out of the total self and cannot be persuaded, argued, fussed, or threatened into being. Perhaps to mention a few will not be harmful, and might serve as guidelines toward growth. The most nearly universal traits of great teachers, in my judgment, are these: (1) Integrity or authenticity: a freedom from phoniness or pretense, an approach to genuineness and utter sincerity. (2) Enthusiasm or zest: an ardent belief in the significance of what one is doing and the energy to put life into it. (3) Directness or nearness to reality: a trait manifested in an almost childlike relation to things and people, an elemental quality of immediacy that escapes the deadening, heavy hand of pedantry and overabstraction. (4) Perspective or length and breadth of view: manifested frequently in a sense of humor, patience, freedom from the scourge of perfectionism. (5) Freedom of mind, especially freedom of imagination: a trait that encourages ideas to flow freely, an eagerness to consider many alternatives. (6) Breadth of interest or sensitivity to a wide spectrum of life: manifested in wide reading and varied concerns. (7) An abiding concern for the individual learner: an ability to feel and communicate the notion that the individual learner is significant, that he has potential of great worth and that it can be realized.

More fundamental than any list of attributes or traits (which at best can only be illustrative) is the principle that the effective teacher must be alive and growing. This growth must be taking place in two great dimensions of personality and character: knowing and being.

No mortal, teacher or not, will reach or even approach the highest ideals of knowing and being. To reach them is not the purpose or even the hope. Here, as almost everywhere in life, it is not the goal but the going toward the goal that counts for most. Therefore, the most effective guide to learning must himself be engaged in genuine learning. A learning journey that to the guide is a stale, meaningless, uninteresting job to be done will be, or will soon become, a like experience to the student. A learning journey that to the guide (whether in kindergarten or university) is fresh and alive, as a journey first taken, will be fresh and alive to learners. Growth in knowledge and in quality of being is the essence of the life which gives life to all learning.

PART TWO

Wider Horizons for Excellence

Introduction: Wider Horizons

Earl V. Pullias
Aileene Lockhart

Education of the future will require that teaching be imaginatively conceived. Teaching-learning at its best is a distinctly creative process. In formal education, the bright essences of the process often have been diluted, and that which rightly is healing and growth-producing has become hurtful and growth-hindering for both teacher and taught.

In writing this book, we have wished to enrich the conception of the matchless art of teaching — to lift it out of narrow and dull pedantry into which it often falls and place it in a framework of continuous growth toward excellence. In the first part we have tried to suggest what the higher learning is about, and hence what the guidance of learning at the college level should be. Then we have attempted to describe a few goals and means for excellence in teaching. Aware of the infinite complexity of this topic and of how very little is known about it, we have presented these thoughts and feelings as tentative suggestions in

47

the spirit of sharing and searching with fellow-teachers who also may be seekers for wisdom and skill in these matters.

Perhaps we should have been satisfied with the presentation of the general vision as we see it, and resisted the temptation to extend the odyssey. But our conception of teaching demands further exploration. The purpose of the second part of the book is thus to explore some of the often neglected regions which are vitally related to excellence in college teaching. The emphasis is upon the exploratory nature of these essays. We know that we cannot begin to map fully the areas we touch. Our purpose is to suggest wider horizons to ourselves and to other teachers who long to grow toward excellence; our hope is to stir thought and stimulate search, not to provide answers or set minds at rest.

It seems to us that this way to excellence — this realization of the fullest potential of teaching—implies a special kind of growth in personality, in value judgments, in creativity, in critical thinking and in interpersonal relations. This process involves deeply and intimately both travelers on the learning journey: teacher and student. There are certainly other aspects of teaching excellence, but these have been chosen as important examples of the wider dimensions of college teaching so vital to the conception of teaching we wish to suggest. These essays are submitted as a beginning or starting point for fellow teachers who have a taste for the adventure of exploration. It would be the hope of each of the five college teachers who had a part in preparing this section of the book that these initial observations might stir others to thought and action that would be better than any one of us has yet been able to achieve. Perhaps the fondest hope of every teacher is that those who study with him will go beyond him in all things.

Toward
Critical Thinking

Aileene Lockhart

Search for improvement characterizes education today but there is real danger in limiting our efforts to intellectual achievement alone. The teacher's task becomes an overpowering one if education is conceived as a total quality affecting all "the uses of life." We cannot plow only one acre; we cannot remain neutral to the need of all men for compassion and charity and understanding. Believing that a community of scholars must be dedicated to a broad concept of excellence and that higher education is not meeting its total obligation to society unless wide dimensions are encompassed, in these pages we have isolated for exploration six large aspects of excellence, the development of which appear imperative to a proper kind of total maturity. Participation as fully awakened citizens requires, at the least, concerted efforts on our part to seek not only growth in knowledge but growth in being and growth in human relationships. It demands also efforts to develop creative and critical abilities to the limits set by nature for each individual, and it forces recognition that teachers are not only concerned with but are committed to the development of value judgments. Growth in all these aspects is the aim of education. Each of these forms of excellence, none of which is likely to be outdated by time and each of which is necessary for complete human dignity and integrity, is considered separately herein. The present chapter is devoted to one of these, the development of critical thinking.

A definition of "critical," the one no doubt implied in the term *critical thinking,* is "that which is characterized by careful analysis, an attempt at objective judgment to determine both merits and faults." And "thinking," according to that customary source of definition, Webster, consists of "thoughtful, reflective, rational exercise of the mental faculties [in order to] arrive at conclusions." Critical thinking then is unclouded thinking and results in commitment reached after logical thought.

Intelligence in the widest sense is a multifaceted thing; no single ability is responsible for its diverse functioning. According to J. Paul Guilford, the eminent psychologist who has spent more than thirteen years studying the mysterious architecture of the human intellect, man's mind has at least three faces: the figural (perceived through the senses); the symbolic (composed of letters, signs, and symbols); and the semantic (involving abstract verbal meanings or ideas and factors commonly called creative and critical). Indeed in attempting to isolate some of the mind's unique capabilities, Professor Guilford has concluded that man may be endowed with more than 120 different intellectual abilities. There are verbal intelligence and spatial intelligence. There are abilities which enable us to discover information, others to produce new information; there are some that allow us to memorize. As a matter of fact, there are different kinds of memory—memory for symbols, words, and details. There are abilities which make possible the recognition of symbols. There are evaluative abilities, and many others. Fortunately, most persons possess many such basic abilities in varying amounts. And, happily, a growing person can acquire many of these, or at least improve them to some extent with practice. So it is possible to learn to think effectively, in short, critically. There are ways to think clearly, but to learn to do so takes discipline and practice.

Critical thinking involves the use of a system of values (a search for the verifiable truth) by which we determine choices, and a system of searching for these values. Critical thinking is the judicial part of our cerebration. It implies controlled thought, action, or judgment based on logic rather than on feeling. It demands the processes of comparing and discriminating, distinguishing, finding coherent relationships. . .finding similarities and discrepancies between alternatives. It involves analyzing. It entails selecting and deferring. It requires moving from premises to conclusions in a logical manner. The critical thinker does not hug to himself the first answer that he comes upon. He rejects any compulsion to think prescribed thoughts; he recognizes when persuasion alone rather than conviction based on evidence is the basis for decision. The critical thinker attempts to arrive at conclusions and determine values on the basis of reason.

Critical thinking demands an authentic independent spirit and intelligent skepticism. This does not mean a negative, habitual attitude of doubt or deliberate nonconformity. Little will have been accomplished if we exchange habitual belief for habitual disbelief, for we are probably equally well off to accept everything as to reject everything. Nor does critical thinking mean challenging the trivial or engaging in pretentious verbalism or using many words to say nothing at all, all of which are habits that characterize the crooked rather than the straight thinker. These words by Arthur Kudner as reported in *The Saturday Review* seem especially apt:

Little Words
Never fear big long words,
Big words name little things.
All big things have little names.
Such as life and death, peace and war.
Or dawn, day, night, hope, love, home.
Learn to use little words in a big way.
It is hard to do but they say what you mean.
When you don't know what you mean, use big words.
That often fools little people.[1]

The forest is full of tangles and traps. It is necessary to learn to recognize the good as well as the bad, the true as well as the false, the half-false, the distorted, and the dishonest. Critical thinking requires weighing the relative merits of that which is written, or spoken, or thought. It is not argument *per se*, or debate, or an effort to put across a favorite idea, or an attempt to be clever. It is constructive, not destructive. It is responsible and honest, for it is accurately aimed to discover the truth. The critical thinker puts into practice Francis Bacon's credo, "Read not to deny or confute, not to accept and believe, but to weigh and consider."

Straight Thinking

Far from considering myself an authority on logic, being insufficiently equipped in so comprehensive a field, I have long speculated, nevertheless, on the nature of critical thinking, believing this ability vital to our existence as well as a contributor to our pleasure. With complete acknowledgment of a debt to many but with full personal responsibility for inadequacies, here are hazarded presently held results of observation, reflection, and study. What is critical thinking? Stated in the simplest terms, the fundamental premise presented here is that critical thinking is straight thinking; it is relevant thinking, and the terms "critical," "clear," and "straight" can be used interchangeably. Despite the possibility that this process has some characteristics of a "seamless coat" and cannot be comprehended completely, it does seem possible to pick out general patterns of action that result in effective thought. Obviously we shall not go very deeply here; it is evident that only an outline of the principles involved can be touched upon.

What does a person do when he thinks clearly? First, he singles out the *major* issues by distinguishing between the significant and the trivial. He tries to define the problem explicitly, unequivocally. Narrowing an issue to its skeletal form is necessary for critical thinking; in fact, without a clear idea of what we are dealing with, fact-gathering will avail nothing. To define is to outline the boundaries and to describe as exactly as possible the characteristics of an issue; to define also is to distinguish an issue from others with which it might be confused.

To put a problem in an appropriate frame so that it can be seen distinctly is a task that cannot be evaded. Is the question stated plainly? The clear thinker tries to bore straight to the point. He tries to hit the center of the target. Until the main point is identified, the relevance of all that surrounds it cannot be seen in true perspective. In more usual terms, the critical thinker first recognizes and defines the problem. This he attempts to accomplish objectively and without bias. He never assumes that the first source consulted provides the only answer, much less a complete answer, or the right answer.

The straight thinker next recognizes underlying assumptions. He tries to reduce their number to the minimum. Issues have antecedents and rest on bases sometimes solid, sometimes not. It is always necessary to examine carefully the conditions which have a bearing on the problem. Without an understanding of the base, there is no logical starting place, no recognizable spot from which to proceed, no firm background for evaluation. Parenthetically, it is difficult to differentiate precisely between the processes of rational thinking and evaluation. Each demands the judgment of the other with no marked line between the two, though the latter extends beyond the former.

The good thinker marshals *all* the evidence. He checks authoritative sources for information and mobilizes all of his own appropriate knowledges and ideas. He then scrutinizes all of these. He recognizes the human tendency to place unbounded faith on his own limited personal experience; he knows that it is easy to assume that because "this" happened to me or mine, it happens to everyone, so he avoids such unwarranted generalizations. The good thinker attempts with all his might to distinguish between what he knows and what he may be taking for granted. He puts little faith in a conclusion drawn solely from documentation consciously or unconsciously selected merely to "prove the point." Suppression of evidence and failure to consider *both* sides of the coin are dishonest, intolerable practices for those who try to think straight. Evidence, all the evidence, is "the starting point of certitude in every order of thinking."[2]

The effective thinker questions what he reads and hears and sees and feels. He learns to ask insightful and meaningful questions: questions about origins, about relationships, about causes, and about values. The great philosophers have posed important questions. Perhaps logical analysis begins with Socrates' query "What does this mean?" and proceeds with Aristotle's "Why?" and Galileo's "How?" When so questioning, the straight thinker's aim is directed toward a clear hit on the target, toward getting as near the truth as possible—not, craftily, toward trying to trip, and not with any concealed pretense calculated to make himself appear wise. Repeated and precise thought about "What is the point?" pays off. Profitable questioning is apt to result after the issue first has been isolated accurately and after appropriate respect has been paid to the cues which present themselves while searching for all the evidence. "Isidor Isaac Rabi [one of America's outstanding physicists] became a scientist, he says, for one overpowering reason: 'I couldn't help it.' Brought to this country as an infant, he has never forgotten his mother's daily query when he came home from public school on Manhattan's Lower East Side: 'Did you ask any good questions today?' "[3] Those interested in the *Art of Asking Questions* should examine a most readable little book by that title written by Stanley L. Payne.

The clear thinker determines what is meant by the words that are used. He seeks precise definitions for key terms when such precision is appropriate. He is unimpressed by gobbledygook lingo or pretentious jargon. Neither is he influenced by stereotypes and clichés. The seldom-questioned comforts of conventionality and the warm familiarity to the trite—neither lulls the critical thinker to sleep. His is no parrot-brain. "It is precisely upon those things we tend to 'take for granted,' " says Ashley Montagu, "that we need from time to time to hang the biggest question marks."[4] The clear thinker, consequently, listens to those who do not agree with him. He listens to those who do not understand him. In so doing he may discover bases for confusion or loopholes in his own thinking.

The critical thinker distinguishes between fact and unsupported opinion, between the verified and the unverified. In addition, he distinguishes among varying degrees of verifiability. The critical thinker also recognizes that when he and others display great confidence, it is probably time to investigate the bases for such confidence. He knows that where there is emotional content, rational thinking is apt to cease, but he realizes that "it is not emotion that annihilates the capacity to think clearly, but the urge to establish a conclusion in harmony with the emotion and regardless of the evidence."[5] Highly recommended to those who wish to learn to detect and to avoid illogicalities is a little paperback book by Susan Stebbing called *Thinking to Some Purpose*.

The critical thinker practices restraint. He avoids making hasty judgments. He withholds decision if the evidence is confused. Never does he disagree merely for the sake of disagreement, nor does he put forth opposing arguments until he understands the point being made. In other words, he tries to know the entire cluster of conditions before coming to a conclusion.

What does a person do when he thinks critically? He distinguishes between the relevant and the irrelevant; he notes that which is discordant with, as well as that which agrees with, the assumptions. Central issues are clothed with definitions, with illustrations, with comparisons, and with observations. Are these truly and closely related to the main problem? Are they of equal pertinence? Of equal significance? Are they essential to understanding, or do they confound the picture? Are they adequate? Do they help to guide the inquiry, help it move with continuity? The critical thinker sorts and classifies his information, and checks to see if each bit is in accord with the whole and if each bit fits without conflict into its niche. If it does not do so, he recognizes either that he has not found all of the facts or that his hypothesis is in error. It may be seen, then, that the critical thinker organizes his facts, including all those that have a bearing on the problem, so that successive relationships, important interrelationships, and contradictions stand out. He strains out matters that are simply diverting. By simplifying, by separating, and by measuring the relative importance of that which is left, he is able to stick to the point.

Finally after he has assessed the facts, analyzed the situation, and marshalled all the "findings" the critical thinker decides whether a conclusion is warranted by the evidence, if it neatly draws together into one fabric all the threads of that which preceded it, if it represents a logically inferred fruition of the findings. Whenever possible, he checks his logic by measurement.

A conclusion is a generalized climax toward which every link in the chain of reasoning points. Its general applicability should be tested. But our critical thinker is always careful not to stretch a conclusion to a point beyond its pertinence for this extension would, of course, expand an otherwise logical conclusion to a fallacious one.

In spite of apparent rigidity in the machinery of critical thinking, the clear thinker is a flexible thinker; he changes his views in accordance with the evidence. In spite of apparent inflexibility in technique, critical thinking makes possible the freedom to think and the independence of mind which constitute the essence of higher education in any age. Paradoxically, some restriction is necessary in order to achieve all that freedom offers.

Crooked Thinking

It is self evident that the crooked thinker engages in practices opposed to those presented in the foregoing. Perhaps it may be helpful, however, to point out briefly some of the habits that are inimical to critical thinking. What are the pitfalls? What customs operate against effective thought? Referring again to *Thinking to Some Purpose* we learn that

Some of the obstacles that impede us [are] : *the difficulty of resisting propaganda and of being content to be persuaded where we should have been convinced, the difficulties of an audience dominated by an unscrupulous speaker and the difficulties of a speaker who has to address an audience that is lazy and uncritical—in short, the difficulties created by our own stupidity and by those who take advantage of that stupidity. Finally there is the difficulty of obtaining information—the difficulty of knowing how to discover reliable testimony.*[6]

Other practices previously mentioned also mitigate against clear thinking: letting the emotions become the basis of judgment instead of evidence; attacking a person instead of a principle; letting irrelevant or unproved evidence become the basis for conclusion; suppressing or distorting any evidence; looking only at the evidence that supports one's view; and attaching a casual relationship between the before and after—that is, ascribing an unjustified associational relationship or assuming that a relationship is one of cause and effect.

Crooked thinking, then, is biased thinking. It may result from basic inability to think straight, but in college students it is more likely to result from laziness, from poor practices which have become habitual, from superficiality, or from a closed mind.

Satisfaction with mediocrity is a condition in which critical thinking cannot live. So is the absence of an inquiring spirit, or the passive acceptance of the cut and dried. It should be noted by all those interested in the development of excellence that pedantic teaching is a deadly corrosive preventing the development of independent, clear thought.

Growth in Ability to Think Critically

Even for those who have cultivated the steps which critical thinking requires, there are many obstacles in our "homogenized society" which mediate against it: pressures of standardization; suggestion of propaganda and advertising; the impact of technology; prevalence of complacent satisfaction with mediocrity; efforts toward the subjugation of ideas; progressive tendency toward conformity and uniformity; widespread prejudices and tensions, anxieties and fears; the search for security and tranquility; the passivity engendered by the appalling expansion of knowledge; the development of psychological methods for behavior control and efforts toward control of the mind.[7] Never has it been more urgent for man to think critically. To develop both cognitive and rational excellence is a crucial challenge of our era. What can we do through teaching to develop the necessary skills of critical thinking so that tomorrow's citizenry can use critical thought not only in positions of power and responsibility but in the course of everyday living? "Everyman" must learn to think as critically as he is able.

Development of critical thinking is essential to the achievement of the two purposes of higher education discussed in Chapter 1: to transmit the culture from one generation to the next so that we can profit from all man has learned, and to aid in the never-ceasing search for and discovery of previously unknown truths. Critical thinking is necessary to the first of these objectives in order to enable us to distinguish, from the mass of that accumulated, that which culturally *is* the best mankind has achieved. The requirement of critical thinking in the latter, search and discovery, is self-evident.

The ability to think critically does not necessarily come naturally. The seed of questioning, of weighing alternatives, of deferring judgment, of reaching sound conclusions has to be nurtured, and sometimes planted. It does not automatically emerge and is slow growing. We must educate for it purposefully and by design. The seed of critical thinking has to be cultivated and tended and nourished and exercised. Exercise is as necessary for the mind as for the muscles. The process takes time, it takes practice, it takes patience, it takes understanding, it requires effort, it demands courage. And, above all, it takes the supporting basic belief that critical thinking is *worth* developing and *can be developed.*

Since convictions speak more eloquently in action than in words, probably the chief thing that teachers can do to develop critical thought in students is to practice critical thinking themselves. In so doing they supply a stimulus and example, and provide an atmosphere which encourages and sustains students in their efforts toward critical thought. Students are very much affected by what is demonstrated for them and what is expected of them. It will net us little to expect that which is foreign to our own conduct. But if critical thinking is demonstrated by the faculty, if teachers demand of themselves that which they endeavor to develop in others, the spirit is contagiously and enthusiastically caught by students. This Edmund Sinnot calls "the contagion of intimacy," and Ernest Dimnet adds in a most challenging book which all teachers should devour, *The Art of Thinking,* that "Nobody denies [that we] gain by being drunk at the spring. . . .Produce favorable conditions and you produce the art of thinking."[8]

That everyone can be taught to think effectively may be quite open to question, but certainly students who have reached the college level can be aided in extending this ability. What are the conditions for its development? The first requisite was seen to be *example.* Both critical and creative abilities are crippled by pedantic and authoritarian teaching. A second requisite is the provision of a suitable *atmosphere,* for minds grow best when the climate is best. This means that there must be freedom: freedom *from* the commonplace; freedom *from* the methodized, the systematized; freedom *from* dogmatism. There must be freedom: freedom *to* propose ideas and subject them to logical examination; freedom *to* be in error; freedom *to* observe, reflect, discover, search, speculate, evaluate. There must be humility; there must be openmindedness; there must be flexibility.

A third requisite is called practice, *exercise. All* ideas should be subject to appraisal. Just as one learns any skill, one learns to think: when guided but not coerced in one direction, when practice is conducted under favorable learning conditions, when one sees the reasons for practice, when progress is rewarded. Experience plays a large role in learning. The student has a right to expect encouragement, a right to expect example, a right to expect the opportunity to develop his own abilities.

It is the student's prerogative to practice his critical and creative abilities in every classroom. There is too much treading water in little, unrelated pools. While we recognize fully that every subject must require its own training and content, methods of thinking are similar. To learn how to think is vastly more important than to learn what to think. Though embarked on a voyage with many navigators, the college student should be able to expect consistency of direction; the journey should be enriched by the unique knowledge of each guide, different scenes being examined along the course with appropriate experts. But there should be only one goal for the journey. All guides should help the learner to stand up and look around for himself and should give him an opportunity to steer the ship. Without practice, without sympathetic guidance, thinking may remain on the rocks.

The imaginative teacher, committed to the idea of developing critical thinking, will devise many means in addition to the following to accomplish his task but these must surely be included among his procedures: Encourage students' asking, and show respect for their questions. Seek all points of view, obtain all the evidence, devote oneself to truth. Apply the test of honesty. Seek clarity, acknowledge differences and difficulties. Subject ideas to scrutiny; ask questions that "dig" (the phrasing of a question influences thinking). Avoid the "yea and nay" response —instead, help students find the evidence, the meaning, the purpose for themselves. Maintain a high level of expectation, thus avoiding standardization, mere competency and conformity, the cliché, and the stereotype. Help students to hold to the point and to recognize relevancy and irrelevancy. Reject triviality and pomposity. Finally, discourage any emphasis merely on "grades," a practice not conducive to the development of critical or creative thinking and opposed to the development of curious, inventive persons.

None of this is intended to imply that the educator should not actively direct learning, for this is his responsibility. Neither does this imply that the teacher should not have his opinions, his preferences, nor that he should not express them. When he does, however, he should give them proper labels; he should cite reasons for his beliefs, and major objections to them should be examined.

If critical thinking is to be contagious, the student must be surrounded by it. The student yearns to be shown by example. Call this indoctrination if you wish; nevertheless, in an atmosphere of example the teaching-learning log becomes highly effective and results in the critical mind. Arthur Little, once president of the American Chemical Society, is reported to have epitomized such a mind as:

> *Having the ability to wonder.*
> *Having the ability to question.*
> *Having the power to generalize.*
> *And the capacity to apply.*

As we move toward excellence through critical thinking, through critical thinking we achieve excellence, and achieve excellence in critical thinking while we are about it. Critical thinking provides a means to give man control of his destiny.

6

Toward Creative Thinking

Donna Mae Miller

The responsibility of higher education is not limited to accumulating and transmitting the embodied knowledge of the past. Sheltering that which has survived through the ages and sifting—evaluating—and synthesizing it are essential functions; but important as these activities are in providing bases from which reasoning and judgment can proceed and perspective be determined, the obligations of the college are only partly and insufficiently discharged thereby. There are additional, inescapable duties and opportunities, among them the necessity for fanning the spark of creativity, stimulating research, continuously seeking *the possible,* and glimpsing the dawn of that which lies *beyond* the present. Within the past decade it has become plainly apparent that higher education must be dedicated to the encouragement of inventiveness, discovery, imagination, and productivity—in short, to creativity. What makes a person creative? What do we know about the creative process and the environment in which it flourishes? What implications can be drawn for the teacher?

The Creative Person

While there is considerable profusion in the variety of definitions and perspectives given to the creative person, it is generally agreed that the capacity to create is no special prerogative of the highly gifted or of the academically talented person, and that the abilities involved can be developed, at least to some degree, in seemingly very diverse fields.

There has long been speculation upon the relationship between intelligence and creativity. Evidently, there are various kinds of intelligence and various kinds of creativity but intellectual factors do contribute to creativity. Recent long-range studies (particularly by J. P. Guilford, professor of psychology at the University of Southern California, and Donald W. MacKinnon, Director of the Institute of Personality Assessment and Research at the University of California in Berkeley) as well as others, have done much to explain the connection between intelligence and creative ability, to change the traditional stereotype of the creative person, and to define aptitudes of creative persons.

Professor Guilford believes that if the term "intelligence" is interpreted broadly it includes the diverse kinds of creativity. It appears that, in general, creativity demands above average mental ability but intelligence in the narrowly conceived customary sense does not assure creativity. There are many factors which comprise that which we call intelligence and persons possess these attributes in various degrees. In a like manner, there are many factors which make up that which we call creativity, and attempts have been made to define the primary traits of creativity. Basic factors identified by Professor Guilford[1] as definitely associated with creative thinking include *fluency* of thinking: ideational, associational, and expressional abilities (the knack of producing many and varied ideas and relationships from stored information); *flexibility*: spontaneous and adaptive flexibility (the ability to produce unusual, divergent, original ideas and directions, and the ability to discriminate); and *elaboration*: or execution (the ability "to arrive at an elaborate, finished product").

Numerous tests have been devised by Professor Guilford to measure various "faces of intellect" and to analyze components of different kinds of intelligence. Typical questions used to explore fluency require a person to produce spontaneously as many responses as possible to a prescribed situation, such as naming objects which are round, hard, and edible, and listing synonyms and antonyms for the word "hard." Representative questions used to measure flexibility require the examinee, for example, to list uses for the common brick, to give titles for a story plot and captions for cartoons. Other measures require drawing a variety of implications from given information, and solving problems which demand improvisation and elaboration. The psychologist-devisor of these tests says:

Realization that the more conspicuously creative abilities appear to be concentrated in the divergent-thinking category, and also to some extent in the transformation category, we may now ask whether we have been giving these skills appropriate exercise. It is probably true that we need a better balance of training in the divergent-thinking area as compared with training in convergent thinking and in critical thinking or evaluation.[2]

Since creativity apparently results from specialized powers, and since intelligence itself is a multi-dimensional phenomenon, the person with a high Intelligence Quotient may or may not possess to a high degree those factors which are associated with creative ability. Whereas many creative persons show wide interests and broad knowledge, others display highly developed but narrow interests and abilities. Those concerned with the preservation and development of creativity should be wary of attempting to make all persons into well-rounded, completely adjusted individuals. Educators are advised to develop all the talents of a student as much as possible but, by all means, to "accent the positive." We are endowed apparently with some amount of each of the facets of intelligence and each factor can be developed to some extent, but the main contributions which a person is potentially capable of making lie in the area of his native basic strengths.

Certain nonintellectual as well as intellectual factors are also involved. Creative persons are distinguished in several modalities of personality. They are more independent than conforming, more complex than placid; they are highly perceptive and possess broad ranges of curiosity, self-confidence, maturity, drive, and energy. They are unusually fluent and flexible. Openness to new experiences, coupled with far-reaching genuine interests, lack of repression, and high motivation make them authentically independent persons. With distinctly developed abilities of observation and retention, they thereby automatically possess a wide source of raw material. This they are able to transform and recombine in innumerable unique ways to solve problems or to suggest novel approaches and untried relationships.

Personal attributes such as self-confidence, impulsiveness, attitude, alertness, and strong motivation are important to creative production. Creative persons are interested and, consequently, interesting persons. They combine tenacity with enthusiasm and great curiosity.

Creative persons are able to see oblique relationships and to draw diverse implications; they are not troubled by unimportant details. Since they avoid obvious and customary approaches to problems, we label them as "ingenious." Professor McKinnon has concentrated upon defining traits which characterize the highly creative and has found that such a person reveals himself by

. . .*his openness to experience, his freedom from crippling restraints and impoverishing inhibitions, his esthetic sensitivity, his cognitive flexibility, his independence in thought and action, his high level of creative energy, his unquestioning commitment to creative endeavor, and his unceasing striving for solution to the ever more difficult problems that he constantly sets for himself.*[3]

Creative persons are independent. They avoid the cult of sameness. In the past, innumerable conditions too often may have blunted the edge of excellence in individual performance. One wonders about the effect of dead-level equality in those learning situations in which the friendship pattern is highly emphasized through much use of sociograms. One questions the advisability of resorting too frequently to group decisions, committee responsibility, and cooperative learning. Neither the classroom nor the playfield can be approached as a vast arena where all should start and end evenly in the race. Perhaps we have devised rather elaborate arrangements for levelling differences in performance partly because of misguided interpretation of the meaning of democratic equality and partly because we have preferred not to discuss students' limitations of ability. At any rate, William Buckley reminds us in *Up From Liberalism* that if you "socialize the individual's surplus. . . you socialize his spirit and creativeness; you cannot paint the Mona Lisa by assigning one dab each to a thousand painters."[4] Cooperative "brainstorming" may result in a quantity of ideas but their quality may not be high. Solitude is a prerequisite to the highest levels of creativity.

A relationship between conflict and complexity and the capacity to be creative receives support from various sources. "Conflicts," says Erich Fromm, "are the source of wondering," and Paul Tillich adds that "it becomes. . . destructive if the risk of insecurity, imperfection, and uncertainty is avoided." There are dangers to the development of curiosity and imagination when persons are spared the experience of conflict through competition. A slight sense of uncertainty and lack of direction cause tension, a prerequisite to spontaneity, and a condition in which a freely questioning mind, captivated by curiosity, thrives.

One cannot discuss the dangers to the creative spirit by over-socialization without considering its counterpart, conformity, as an obstacle to creative thinking. Creativity may not be developed or retained in classrooms where rigidity, conformity, organization, and routine are the rule; in such situations docility and passivity are rewarded rather than indepedence. Conformity in behavior may be a human necessity but conformity of thought and patterns of thought is a human danger.[5] Creativity thrives best in climates of personal freedom and nonconformity of ideas. Creativity demands active involvement and unconventional approaches so is stunted in conditions of conformity. The highly creative plow both ends of a field rather than cultivating the middle alone. The popular belief, however, that those who are truly highly creative are Bohemian in all regards is a mistaken one; often these persons are quite conventional in matters outside of their areas of talent. Their nonconformity is exhibited within the realm of their ideas and their approaches to problems.

The Creative Process

In the numerous books and articles describing the creative process which have been published within the past ten to fifteen years, four stages commonly are recognized: (1) the stage of saturation or total immersion in the subject; (2) the mental digestive stage where there is interaction of ideas; (3) the period of incubation of ideas; and (4) the birth or inspiration stage. This categorization is an artificial and imperfect one for often the periods overlap or do not occur in sequence and, whereas some of the process may be engaged in consciously and deliberately, much of it may be subconscious.

The latter stage, inspiration, is rarely achieved without the others. In any event, complete immersion in the subject seems necessary. Saturation with the subject, that is, preparation without too much critical evaluation, is an important prerequisite for creative thought. It is obligatory to be prepared, but saturation must be accompanied by enthusiasm, for freshness for the subject must be maintained.

The dedication which complete immersion in an idea requires demands discipline. The teacher who provides no direction or evaluation does not foster fine work. Architect Allen Dow, a contributor to *Creativity and Its Cultivation,* tells of hearing a ballet master admonish his pupils by saying, "Please remember that naturalness is not art." Shoddiness must never be accepted in the name of creativity. Superior results must be sought and cherished. Regardless of individual ability, each must *strive* for excellence because, as John Gardner so aptly states in a recent book by that title:

An excellent plumber is infinitely more admirable than an incompetent philosopher. The society which scorns excellence in plumbing because plumbing is a humble activity and tolerates shoddiness in philosophy because it is an exalted activity will have neither good plumbing nor good philosophy. Neither its pipes nor its theories will hold water.[6]

Implications for Education

Assumptions agreed upon by those working on the intriguing aspects of creativity are: all persons possess some creative potential; this potential can be developed; the nature and process of creativity can be understood. It must be remembered that creativity is not just one ability; many talents and qualities contribute to inventiveness and productivity. Without these assumptions no attempts would be made to devise and evaluate methods of teaching aimed at the development of creative potential. There is, however, sufficient evidence to indicate that aspects of a generalized concept of creativity can be improved. Outstanding examples of training centers where methods are being fashioned are located at the University of Buffalo and the University of Minnesota. Improvement can be made in using such abilities as do exist, but of course no training method can develop that which is not basically inherent.

Some implications of creativity research for the educator are interwoven in the discussion so far presented. Let us dwell briefly now on further suggestions. It is known that there is a substantial relationship between a wide vocabulary and creative thought. It would seem helpful to saturate the student with both verbal and nonverbal skills, the intricacies of the language of mental and physical activity, for both can be effective vehicles of thought and expression. In a delightful little book, *A Technique for Producing Ideas,* James Young writes, "Words are, themselves, ideas. . . in a state of suspended animation. When the words are mastered the ideas tend to come alive. . . we can collect ideas by collecting words."[7]

There probably is wisdom then in using word-study and analogy as a means of increasing the capacity for originality and articulate expression. A student in an archery class, for example, encouraged in the exciting adventure of word use, conceived the following idea:

The bow and arrow, symbol of archery everywhere, I picture as this: the BOW represents one's self, the ARROW, the means by which we reach our goals. The NOCK is the meeting place of one's aims and one's self. The FLETCHING, I conceive as a pilot or stabilizer in life and moral thought in all we do. The CREST on the arrow is the emblazoned heritage of ideas, bright around the shaft of the arrow so that we may identify ideals. The PILE, that part which touches the target first, is the advance hint of one's creative thought; the SHAFT follows into the target on impact, bringing home our ideas to their goal.[8]

The use of words which are simple, clear, and specific make not only the expression of ideas but their very productivity possible. This generalization can be extended to the precise mastery of other symbols appropriate to other media. . . numbers, notation, color, movement, and so on.

The mind must have available the raw materials with which to work. Before one can be truly creative he must be prepared with a workable understanding of his medium and must develop not only its technique but flexibility in handling it. It is impossible to contribute to mathematical theory with no understanding of mathematics. The educator who wishes to develop creativity in his students must see that basic knowledges and skills are mastered. It follows that even the most energetic teacher must have more than ordinary mastery of his medium before he can develop the insight of his students to any valuable extent.

Certain conditions serve as facilitators or inhibitors of the creative attitude. The best way to create a climate in which students can develop creativity is to bring them in touch with teachers of distinction, with teachers who themselves display imagination. We tend to become like those to whom we are exposed. Throughout this book emphasis has been placed upon the impact of great teachers. The undeniable value of this association with such teachers is nowhere displayed more prominently than in the development of creativity. The teacher who questions, who tries to find relationships, differences, and analogies, who shows facility in simplifying, elaborating, substituting, varying, and combining; the teacher who shows enthusiasm and appreciation for discovery; the teacher who demonstrates imagination and curiosity and encourages these qualities in others — this teacher by his own attitude and intensity produces conditions in which students can be as creative as they are able. This teacher awakens students' capabilities.

Since everyone has more basic creative potential than he customarily uses, and since creative ability is not highly related to the usually narrowly defined concept of intelligence, it seems appropriate for the educator to try to unleash creative abilities in all students, not just in those who are academically talented or in those who are obviously gifted. He should encourage all students to be themselves and he must freely accept them as such. While he must be careful not to classify just any form of spontaneity as creative, he must be intuitively alert to all evidences of true originality.

Obviously there is need for rigor in dealing with the slippery concept known as creativity because the word has been loosely used, overused, and invested with such a broad range of meanings. Irving A. Taylor[9] grouped the myriad number of different definitions into five value clusters. The progressive levels which resulted are (1) expressive creativity, or sheer spontaneity; (2) productive creativity, or the technical proficiency exemplified by the production of a number of things; (3) inventive creativity, or ingenuity in putting available materials together in new ways for new ends; (4) innovative creativity, or altering a concept; and, lastly, at the highest level of the scale, (5) emergentive creativity, or the expression of radically different concepts. All five levels of creativity should be encouraged and rewarded, with constant effort to move the learner up this progressive scale.

Finally, the teacher always must be aware that all students are not constructed from the same mold. They cannot be motivated in the same way; the same level of results cannot be expected. It is the teacher's responsibility, however, to encourage the development of creativity up to the level of which each is capable. We must expect each individual, regardless of ability, to strive toward excellence. This requires complete commitment, or dedication, and more effort of the spirit and freshness of attitude than mere technique because creativity apparently involves to a very great extent an attitude, a way of looking at things.

Approaches to excellence through creativity cannot be capsuled, or are all speculations regarding its nature necessarily warranted. The concept of creativity presented here, however, leads to the idea that creativity is a way of life, or an attitude toward life, and depends more upon the intensity and flexibility of a person's will than upon the keenness of his intellect. All evidence shows that we must keep alive the capacity for wonder, must demand discipline while preserving imagination, must encourage ourselves and our students to cross over from one medium to another, and must provide a climate in which new ideas are permitted to grow.

Growth in
Human Relationships

Marjorie H. Bond

The good teacher not only fully accepts but promotes full respect for the essential integrity and dignity of all human beings. This dimension of excellence — human relationships — is examined in the following pages. After a brief historical perspective, reasons for interdependence (those which demand good human relationships) are examined. This discussion is followed by a consideration of some problems in human relating and some suggestions for improved practice in this area.

Often we look to the Greek way for that inspiration of spirit which is needed for our day. In the utterances of Pericles we note perhaps the first defense of social tolerance. Both Socrates and Plato spoke of the mindset which encourages all points of view as a requisite for the preservation of individual freedom. Freedom for personal action was conceived by Pericles; to this Plato added the ideas of intellectual and contemplative freedom. The kind of greatness described by these Greek writers was exemplified in some of the actions of Alexander the Great. As is commonly the case when more facts are brought to bear, there has arisen today a new projection of that young conquering ruler. A truer perspective of this man, who at thirty-three years held authority over much of the civilized world of that early day, can be seen if we look beyond the conquests of battle and heed his strivings to unite mankind.[1]

It is well known that Alexander appointed as territorial governors two non-Greeks. He permitted his own adoption by a native queen. There were occasions when he appeared in public wearing Persian dress, perhaps suggesting to the Greeks that other people were important to him, and to the barbarians that he was their king too. Apparently antagonistic toward the attitude which automatically made barbarians into natural enemies, Alexander accepted these outsiders as partners.

While these acts were useful to Alexander in conquering the world, nevertheless a new concept of relationship was demonstrated. In the third century B.C. this idea became the doctrine of the brotherhood of man as preached by Zeno. Later St. Paul envisioned a world with neither Greek nor Jew, bond nor free. What distance have we traveled since that time? Are we yet ready to value the natural rights of human dignity? Is that freedom which allows a contribution to the whole by each according to his peculiarity to be an achievement of man?

Reasons for Interdependence

Life's daily problem increasingly becomes one of dealing with individuals; our present world demands that we live in close interdependence. The tightening of bonds among all nations and races, cultures, classes, and faiths is of the greatest consequence to man. Nations jockeying for a place in the sun, instantaneous communication, individuals claiming dignity and destiny, the reach of space instruments and the refinement of industrial processes — these along with accumulations of poverty and of wealth, of unemployment, of leisure, and of people force upon us today's challenges. We live in a world curtained by iron and bamboo and walled by fear which turns man's face from man, while at the same time a growing proximity demands more understanding, cooperation, and tolerance.

The toleration of differences is lower in our closely integrated society than it was when distance separated these differences. Unless enough of us come to a better understanding of ourselves and are able to heighten and enrich the type of human relating we have with the many affecting our lives, this interdependence will destroy us through conflict of interest and variability of values. Adventuring into our own inner space holds a valuable priority as a requisite for living in today's world, but each personal outlook also needs enlargement so that the limitations of provincial interests which conflict with national and world moral values can be overcome.

Many believe today that the nation whose educational system recognizes both worthiness in variety and a need for cultural interdependence is the nation that will come to exercise the leading influence. As we view our own culture, it appears that we are gaining slowly in such a perspective. There exists for many a desire to learn about the present and the past. Study of non-Western cultures helps to bring about an understanding of other countries' counterparts to the great historical figures who shaped America. Examples of person-to-person democracy being practiced today have heightened our self-concept and country-concept; democracy becomes more salable when it becomes personal. It is possible that we are learning of the judgmental difficulty resulting from the fact of being members of our own nation; in this effort it is imperative that we be honest with ourselves. Our American self-consciousness begets dishonesty when the image becomes of greater consequence than the reality. There is deception in the concept that we are the only teachers and all others the learners. We cannot learn until we become aware that we have something to learn.

Growing concern exists concerning the relatedness of human beings in their work tasks. Business, industry, medicine, the armed forces and education, to name but a few areas, increasingly recognize that personal relating is a factor important to success. Recently an advertising brochure for a national business magazine called attention to a subscription gift which consisted of a set of three books for the executive; these contain advice on skillful job performance relative to (1) managing your business, (2) managing your people, and (3) managing yourself. From this we might deduce a need to give the human variable twice the concern we allot the business factor.

Recent social science investigations point up the desire people have to remain integrated human beings both in the work situation and at home. While time and motion studies once omitted this human problem, industry today admits that "the whole man goes to work." In education there is curiosity regarding relationships. We put the question in many forms. In one institution of higher learning students were requested to name their most influential high school teachers so that appropriate recognition could be given to those outstanding persons. In the reasons given for their choices students placed emphasis on such human qualities as enthusiasm for the subject, inspiration, the ability to influence, and attitude.

An eagerness for growth in the whole of life's experiences is needed. If we resist, there cannot occur within us that flow of interchange between experience and the self which creates the newness of being. It is this continuing personal transformation through growth which seems to bring satisfaction to man and to hold for him the greatest meaning. The transformation is neither a state nor condition, but an on-going process leading in the direction of truth. Operative among men and between a man and his experience, interchange also can function between countries.

The greatest good is found in an excellence of relationships, and depends upon the full self-giving of individuals in association to "that kind of interchange between each and other which expands and enriches what each can know, feel, and control."[2] Experiential sensitivity allows for a changing meaning, not just adjusting the self or adapting to the situation.

Historically, conflict has most often resulted in domination or compromise. In either case, there is loss which affects all. There is, however, a third alternative — integration. Out of the "dissolution of habitual patterns in the association of ideas" of which Remy de Gourmont speaks, mutual interchange permits new creation. Integration is the organization of various points of view into a new harmonious whole; it results in perception of a totality. Creative results become possible when both sides take directions from the situation and not from each other. By stripping away preconceptions, by looking beyond personalities, there is permitted a closer, truer view. Understanding may result when newly integrated ideas emerge from a creative approach to conflict.

Problems in Human Relating

Perhaps the chief problem we encounter in human relating exists in communication. By substituting a different term for "human relations" there might well occur an improved exchange of meaning. Let this term be "politeness," the opposite of rudeness. It is an old-fashioned, simple word giving high regard for another's dignity, for his individual merit, and for the kind of self-fulfillment which grows from successful interchange. Politeness requests a respect for another's thinking and invokes a hesitancy to invade his secret vulnerabilities. A certain amount of individual containment seems to be suggested for peaceful coexistence. As we share our common predicament in this uncertain world, by example we can teach young people this humble form of tolerance: courtesy and good manners. Politeness implies patience, and excellence in learning takes time for the learner and the teacher. Politeness is tolerance applied on the level of everyday life.

Living in today's double postured world is far from simple, for competition and brotherly love do not make the closest of bedfellows. Our outer and inner worlds put up resistances to the free interchange which could satisfy and build. The world outside the individual encourages the concealment of one's own identity, tending to shape the mind into evasiveness. It becomes easy to permit others to do our thinking for us, and hatred may replace intelligent thought. Your differences of opinion to me become prejudice, while my own stand as true convictions. *This* we come to believe, for we have trusted our thinking to another mind.

Within ourselves the psyche serves as protector from the hurt that may come when sensitivities are exposed in the give-and-take of the interchange process. We fear to reveal something of ourselves and so remain content to deal with life at arm's length. Conflict arises between that individual craving for personal transformation and the protection devised along the route. Not by conforming and so avoiding that inalienable right to think, but rather as we permit ourselves and others the unexpected "out-reach" can we contribute our most.

Practicing Good Human Relations

What concern ought the college teacher have for the foregoing? Professional competence demands a conviction concerning the function of change in the education of students. The teacher must be alert to the multiple causes of change which he himself, other people, and the subject matter are able to effect. He ought to intend to make certain influences, and be prepared to assume responsibility for their occurrence. Moral development, for example, is a pertinent and serious youth need which is strengthened when the individual learns to deliberate over a choice as he sees that choice influencing others as well as himself. Growth in moral behavior can be influenced positively when the range of choice is broadened, the impact of choice studied, and the outcome of choice experienced. Actions may be changed when a better way can be discerned.

Two related factors markedly affect the success of the learning process. Since in a particular sense one learns only to that degree which he allows himself to learn, learning must be given permission by the student. The teaching-learning relationship and learning atmosphere together help to determine how widely the student opens the door. Those teachers with the greatest impact upon their students are the ones who expect and demand much, extending this high level of expectation into their personal contact with students. The teaching-learning relationship ought to develop to a stage wherein it becomes vibrant with the excitement of learning and the freedom for exploration of new ideas. This is possible only in a climate that functions without personal threat. Here students find they can drop their defenses and face the change and growth of learning. Support becomes the keynote; it is up to the teacher to accept all pupils emotionally for the self-concept is affected whether or not we consciously teach with this in mind. Mark Hellinger once admonished us to "find that quality to like or admire, and base our relationship on that." The first task of the teacher then is to establish satisfactory human relations with class members by showing an active interest in them as persons, by showing a concern for their problems, and by believing in their potentialities for creative action. Students might even return such a compliment!

Learners seem to react most favorably to our teaching when we are able to nurture a spirit of interchange. A cooperative atmosphere is one of involvement which can give reason to being and to value in perception. Such growth is a very personal thing. It is not easy for an individual to grow unless there exists a freedom within and a freedom with others. An eagerness for friendly relationships allows for exposure to the true quality in people, provided integrity and self-esteem are preserved in the association.

Learning is fostered in a nonjudgmental atmosphere where individuals may evolve their own values and convictions with increasing perceptual clarity. At first there ought to exist freedom with an idea; spontaneous expression contributes to the growing self. Meaning cannot develop fully in the presenec of fear. To achieve free-flowing interchange, the questions and reactions of students must be accorded utmost respect. Sometimes the teacher aids by self-expression and at other times by restraint. Then ideas must be tested against other active minds and against standards. The communication of an idea becomes an extension of it, with the formulation of new perceptions which occur through the integrating process of reaction with another mind. It is scarcely possible to go all the way alone. Excellence in the teaching-learning relationship will encourage students to uncover for themselves that which has personal meaning for life and behavior.

Teachers must have a sensitivity about their personal impact upon the learning state. Perceptions compose the fabric out of which human relationships are made. To students we are not what we may believe ourselves to be; rather it is their feelings about us with which they must deal, and feelings may be contributive or inhibitory to learning. An excellent book on teacher personality is the 1962 A.S.C.D. Yearbook, *Perceiving, Behaving, Becoming.*[3]

Feelings may come from many habit patterns. Silence communicates quite as clearly as words, for pause gives meaning to our word patterns in much the same way as spacing brings meaning to rhythmic patterning. Body postures, tension, facial expressions, and movement gestures all relay our secret thoughts. Research has shown that gestures are interpreted at a level exceeding that of chance; indeed nonverbal language is apt to be very outspoken. The crisp reply, the hurried response, the irritated intonation may carry with them as much meaning as the words which we so carefully select to convey our intent.

There are many ways of supporting students in their striving toward integration. Joint effort by student and teacher made possible by a network of satisfactory human relationships permits an approach to problem solving and a hope of finding solutions yet unborn. The greater the diversity among the searchers themselves the wider is the range of goal possibility. Human variability appears not only in intelligence, knowledge, point of view, and attitude, but also in race, class, religion, nationality, experience, and the direction of purpose. While we must be discriminatory in our selection of the proper tools for learning, we cannot risk discrimination's mark upon our human relations. To deny the worthiness of a different view is to negate the value of the process of free interchange. Though segregation in the form of ability grouping has a rightful place as a temporary facilitator of learning, there are dangers in the acceptance of complete sameness: superiority and inferiority make difficult an identification with all mankind. To deny public group membership on any basis limits membership in the family of man.

A great injustice lies in stereotyping which, by categorization, insists upon that which is common. To stereotype is to generalize the individual out of existence, and any denial of human capability results in a paucity for mankind. Perhaps the greatest obstacle to satisfactory human relating is our tendency to categorize, to the flourishing of the in-group and the sacrificing of the out-group as a scapegoat. Stereotypes of our perceptions of others often perpetuate a derogatory point of view. Distortions occurring at the original point of contact are subject to multiplication all along the line by speakers and listeners alike. In joke, story, theater drama, or motion picture the tendency is to raise the personal ego by laying blame on the innocent. At minimum these ought to be balanced by some effort to depict the right and proper cultural view. To extirpate the stereotype one should look to the spark of truth upon which the fiction is based and at that point examine where we have disembarked from truth.

Stereotyping in language, in experience, and in thinking, a practice to which we cling for comfort and security, penalizes teaching effectiveness. Inept communication results from impre-

cision in thought often growing out of careless generality. The
correct word must be chosen carefully from our own experience
and that of the listener so that the resultant picture can carry to
the hearer our true intent.

Stereotyped thinking is exemplified also in individuals who refuse to trust their own thinking and so borrow points of view.
Real creativity of thought may be uncommon and all of us live
by others' ideas, but to deal actively with ideas calls for a type
of mental ingenuity. That student who learns only the educational phrasing expected of him expresses the viewpoint of another. As thinking Americans we might avoid the stereotyped
national image we hold of ourselves as omnipotent in all regards,
never second best. It is important to approach matters as they
are seen by others, whether in international or human affairs.
Misunderstandings quickly arise from one side's assuming by
what it says what the other would have meant if it had said it.
When speaking together about ideas it is essential that I not only
hear what you say, but that I listen to you. It might be well to
test myself by repeating your idea to you before I embark upon
my own.

Exposure to variety in people and variety in experiences stimulate growth just as the reverse, limited experience, frequently in-
hibits it. There is wisdom in a wide identification with others, for
one learns to allow for variability. Travel puts us in personal touch with differences throughout the world which we easily accept as right for others, something we find difficult to do
in home territory.

Teaching requires convictions before it can be convincing. The
teacher must have made discoveries about himself, just as now he
is helping the student to make for himself. It is essential to know
something of who and what one is, and where one is going, if
one is to stand before students and lead them. To have an identity, it is important to know to what you belong as well as to what
you do not. Being lost results from being free without knowing
for what, being given the freedom to think but not knowing
where to begin. As teachers accept the process of their own becoming, the student begins to learn to respond to this same process. A freedom to explore the self and others helps us to form a

better image of what we want to become. There is need for the teacher to demonstrate that the search for meaning is worth the effort.

Good teaching can culminate in a creative conversion, a mind change, a total integration. Learning is based not upon what the teacher feels or believes or even knows, but rather on that change which arises out of conflict with previously accepted patterns of action and thought which no longer suffice. Excellent teaching not only makes possible a transmission of the best culture of the past, but also develops the logic of dealing with new types of problems and the ability to make intelligent applications of previously learned facts.

An effort must be made to free the student from all that hinders creative insight. It is at this level that interchange with other generations by study, reading and research, with contemporary counterparts and with specific situations, takes place. Teacher and student together can seek new and harmonious ideas through an application of the principle of integration.

Jerome S. Bruner[4] states that the teacher must permit, even encourage, the commission of error and at the same time provide protection for the learner. Error's consequence is made less grave here than in direct learning for the thoughtful teacher will prepare the student to absorb the shock of error. The teacher acts as a shield, sparing the learner, and error serves its purpose. Mistakes fail to damage when an internal security exists.

Learning and doing have become separated in the process of much of present day education. To be effective, teaching must be accompanied by example. The instructor becomes a model of useful learning when he carries those standards he talks about into his own social and civic life.

The lives of students are subject to growing interdependence on the college campus. Temptation to conform is strong, and for many inescapable. Conformity is found even in the desire to escape its grasp. In those who win out against such odds, a coherent unity of the self is forming. Learning experiences must be included that will give added dimension to the building of qualities which strengthen individuality. The final examination which requires studied insight rather than a feedback of information provides a useful kind of learning.

The art and science of teaching revolves around helping the learner to discover the personal meaning of ideas. Those problems over which there hangs controversy are useful in causing minor upset. Thought can occur when one is stirred and stimulated. Questioning strongly-held concepts has value to the learner. Ideational conflict plays a creative role in education. But there is need to be alert to the stress on objectivity in today's scientific approach to understanding. As we objectify the problem and its solution, we ought not to ignore the influence that results may have upon the learner. The extension of objectivity into a study of community problems will enhance the usefulness of the scientific method for the student.

For learning to mean as much as it might, the learner needs to come into contact with great minds. Too often in our colleges and universities the best teachers are found in full time pursuit of goals other than those which involve the exploration of learning with young people. Since learning is fractional and compartmentalized there exists a need for a unitary approach in order to consolidate meaning. Foundational general education experiences may begin this process. Beyond this first level, core type courses, team teaching, and the master teacher approach can offer the learner a multiple perspective. The interdisciplinary method is utilized best by a number of specialists who have wide understanding. Such a method demands as much successful human relating as it does intellectual power and teaching skill, for learning is easily blighted by human friction.

Reflecting upon the success of Soviet education in providing the type of manpower necessary to manage the affairs of its state, one concludes that perhaps American educators ought to concern themselves with the goals of the American state which include living well with fellow men. The development of good human relations is an inescapable challenge to education. The addition of faculty with a world outlook and students from abroad, both groups of whom represent all economic levels rather than the privileged alone; opportunity to read a variety of first rate newspapers; improvement in language instruction and courses in non-Western culture: this can be a beginning. The world view can permeate art, history, literature, religion, dance— in truth all of education. Increasing contact must be made outside of that familiar, yet confining world, within our own geographical boundaries. Exposure to a world concept should become the privilege of today's educated young people.

Responsibilities outside of teaching require the ability to engender "a fellow feeling." One such function in which all teachers have considerable experience is that of committee work. Let us look at the committee leader and the needed art of conducting a meeting. Courtesy and sense of accomplishment should serve as dual forces giving leverage for action. The leader needs a human quality as much as he needs aptitude in the rules of order. Courtesy eases that sharp edge of power and lessens annoyance in the face of discontent. Generously, courtesy considers the minority group's feeling, and acts to avoid open conflict. It makes sure that all those with something to say are permitted to have that say. A courteous manner on the part of a leader accomplishes much. Through conviction one senses gain, but in compulsion even a real gain becomes less evident.

Who is it who has been assigned the task of helping the student find wholeness of meaning among his fragmented learnings? Someone should be in touch with him long enough to know him as a person. It appears evident that none who teach in the college community dares ignore the obligation to personalize the meaning of learning. Some may be ill-qualified to touch students in large numbers in an intimate way, but each teacher does establish personal contact with some students. It is to these that we can best give guidance. As homage is being paid and training provided for today's mathematics-science major, we should be warned of a need for caution. The possibility of exploitation is great as society, the school, and the parents are all reflecting in his glory. David Reisman[5] urges the teacher to walk a cautious path and implores the school to allow the student to play from weakness as well as strength in his course of studies.

We must keep the human touch. Guidance must be administered gently and moved along with tender steps. Direction is given in thoughtful ways by those who think it important. We are all properly touched by that coach who recognizes the player's spent effort as he walks from the basketball court to his place on the bench, by the gymnastic coach who stations himself as spotter, giving his athletes encouragement and protection. Boys under such fine tuition are rewarded by a high quality of feeling in the kinship of men. There is also the administrator who has developed that consultative relationship which causes his co-workers to seek out his advice rather than to belabor among themselves and with outsiders the dissatisfactions of work. He develops good relationships partly by making someone else's immediate problem his important concern. Finally, that teacher who takes hold of the nub of an idea which a student dares to present, supports, and develops it into something of visible merit is guiding in constructive ways. In all of these examples of providing support the leader is aiding the process of integration within the individual.

One word of caution: there exists imminent danger to an institution just as there does to a people and to a land when concern for the image destroys some of that distance already gained in the observance of man's dignity. Any lowering of standards such as unwisely regarding the undeserving in order to display racial, intellectual, or other forms of tolerance defeats its purpose. Such indignity retards the progress of human relations. The question has been raised as to whether academic excellence must therefore be diluted if a proper view of human relations is to be maintained. There is no conflict. Relationships are but a part of the whole, although they form an aspect of that unity which we neglect at our peril. Academic excellence can be heightened only by the presence of total human excellence; the college-university community must recognize that the human relations dimension cannot responsibly be ignored.

8

Developing
Value Judgments

Marguerite Clifton

Excellence has become a key word descriptive of the goals of Americans. The growing recognition that mediocrity of thought and performance will not sustain a culture fighting to survive in a world of conflicting ideologies gave rise to the urgency for quality. Though every phase of life has been touched by this strong motivating force, perhaps education has felt the greatest impact.

The results have been varied. Students have exhibited an unsuspected quest for knowledge and a tolerance for hard work. Colleges have become increasingly stringent in their selection of potential scholars. Many teachers have delighted in their freedom to focus their energies on students identified as gifted. But, unfortunately, the concept of excellence seems to have assumed a narrow connotation, limited to the sphere of intellectual endeavor. The meaning of excellence certainly must include, in addition, the development of value judgments, for what good will come of knowledge if people are without moral and social principles, without a sense of moral and ethical obligation?

Let us focus our attention on a concept of value, its meaning and sources; examine the college's responsibility for the development of student values; and discuss selected methods for developing and changing values.

A Concept of Value

The impact of a given culture on the future of man is determined by the pattern of beliefs and preferential behavior which it directs toward certain objects and actions as distinctive from others. What does this mean to the individual? Each time he is faced with making a decision he must express preference for one over another possible choice. In so doing, he exhibits his personal preference or "value for" something which then serves to guide his judgment and determine his behavior.

Clyde Kluckholn defines value as:

. . . *a conception explicit or implicit, distinctive of an individual or characteristic of a group, of the desirable which influences the selection from available modes, means, and ends of action.*[1]

Professor Whitehead puts it succinctly by saying values are matters of importance as distinct from mere matters of fact. An individual's values are the result of those facts perceived as central in importance to him. As he gradually develops preferences which serve as criteria for choices we say that he is developing a value system. The constellation of all that he considers worthwhile determines his attitudes and his thoughts and feelings. The individual's expression of a value is a tangible expression of his self-identity. In his recent discussion of personality, Gordon Allport points out that "Personal values are the dominating force in life, and all of a person's activity is directed toward the realization of his values."[2]

A value then is an individual's preferential conception of what is desirable and of greatest importance. His preferences become objectives to be achieved in order to maintain his conception of a happy and satisfying life. Values thus serve as criteria for choices and as guides for selecting courses of action.

"What man actually does with his growing knowledge will depend, not upon that knowledge, but upon man's attitudes, his philosophy, his value judgments." Douglas Lawson,[3] in his *Wisdom and Education*, thus encapsulates the reasons why it is important for each man to identify, question, and strengthen his personal value system. The rapidity of developments in the past decade has all but swept away our stability. Many contemporary historians describe our materialism as the sickness of Western man, and place the blame on the weakness of value commitment in daily operations at the personal, national, and international level. Wavering between values presents serious conflicts for persons living in a democratic culture which has as one of its fundamental beliefs the individual's right to choose between alternatives.

Freedom to choose is the staff of life for every American. Accompanying this privilege is, of course, the moral responsibility to make enlightened choices. For this reason each man must seek a liberal education, one that includes not only factual knowledge, but teaches him the processes of exploring alternatives, applying his concept of the desirable, and making a final free decision. To meet the challenge of the times, man must know *what* he is doing, *why* he is doing it, and actively *direct* changes which are central to him. Acting from personal judgment is a fundamental step in assuming full responsibility for freedom of choice.

The structure and nature of society in the United States provide innumerable subsocieties with which individuals may choose to identify. Each of these subsocieties has a culture; that is, the individuals participating in the group endeavor share certain values and beliefs. These values justify the goals of the group and provide regulations which govern its activity. In order to become a functioning member of a societal group, each person must know what he believes regarding the focus of the group. Though belonging is a need of young people, it assumes less importance for the mature individual. Existing as an individual in a group-structured society is a difficult task at best, but to become a truly contributing member without the guidance of personal value commitment is a near impossibility.

If values are important to direct our lives in a world of conflict, to exercise our freedom, and to strengthen our individual efforts in group endeavors, they are equally necessary to guide us in the attainment of happiness in the form of selflessness. The individual who has developed a system of values that exemplifies truth, goodness, and beauty is not easily upset by the minor disappointments in daily life, and he reveals great strength and resourcefulness in meeting a real crisis. The goals of this individual generally are not immediate, but more often long-range in vision. Possible action is assessed in terms of principles and the effects of action on other people. Behaving in this manner is an ideal goal, one which is probably never completely actualized in an individual's life, but it represents the highest level of moral maturity.

Perhaps no other facet of life has provided man with greater challenge than the questions "What is right and what is wrong?" and "What is good?" These are persistent questions. In his Nicomachean Ethics the philosopher Aristotle noted that there can be no universally accepted idea of good for "There are as many ways of predicating good as of predicating existence."[4] Centuries later, John Stuart Mill in his discourse on utilitarianism recognized that "Some kinds of pleasure are more desirable and more valuable than others."[5] In more recent times, the struggle to identify universal goodness has not ceased.

There exist, however, some generalizations of value which potentially are capable of drawing forth every man's loyalty. Honesty, truthfulness, courage, modesty, and liberality are but a few examples of virtues long considered important. No one would argue with any of these values, but they are operative only to the degree that one can apply the abstract concept to a specific situation. The value of honesty, for example, is an interesting one when considered in the light of the action of college students. The student who would not dream of taking a tie pin from the local haberdashery might permanently "borrow" his fraternity brother's tie pin. While being meticulous about paying for books purchased from the open shelves of the book store, the same student occasionally may "forget" to check out a book that he has taken from the open stacks of the library. Many who would never cheat during a game of tennis practice cheating as an acceptable method of passing an examination. Here we see that honesty, an absolute value, for many is not at all absolute in the operational sense.

Over the centuries, happiness has been considered an ultimate goal of man's existence. The quest for its attainment leads to a consideration of what is needed in order to achieve this goal. This of course produces the age old argument: does one value only what he desires or does he value that which *should* be desired? A struggle appears within each person as a result of his effort to define for himself the meaning of happiness. Youth's lack of experience and vision often limits its search to the narrow confines of immediate goals. When young people begin to identify long range objectives we see this as a sign of reaching toward maturity. This growing maturity leads to the recognition that immediate desire is not necessarily a criterion of ultimate goodness.

If the individual cannot find a rational relationship between *what* he desires and the *ideal* standards that he has learned to value, then his actions may be based on opportunism within a limited field of vision. The young college student who truly values the "ideal" in his choice of a life partner frequently is faced with this conflict. Shall he take advantage of opportunities that will satisfy his immediate desires, or shall his actions support that which he truly values? As the student assumes increasing responsibility for operating on the level of value principle, he gradually develops his own standards and value pattern so that these are no longer mere remnants of his childhood training.

In brief, the greatest value is achieving fullest happiness. In order to accomplish this objective man seeks to identify and exemplify in his life virtues of character that are actually ideal standards governing human conduct. Values which lead to the good life are timeless, universal to a degree, but useful only to the extent that they can be applied to each specific situation. The more nearly an individual observes the principle of altruism, the closer he comes to attaining the goal of his happiness.

Responsibility For Values in the Academic Community

Some observers of the college scene consider it regrettable that so many institutions seemingly are content to reflect the ambiguities of worth characteristic of our age. Two viewpoints are prevalent: the first is that the college's responsibility should be restricted primarily to intellectual attainment; the second holds that the purpose of the college is to stimulate intelligent behavior. Many institutions of higher education unfortunately give lip service to the second viewpoint while actually observing the practices of the first.

The need for identifying the true purposes of higher education is recognized by educators. Many conclude that the university must be the guiding force not only in developing the mind but also in developing the conscience of society. José Ortega highlights this point nicely in one of his closing statements in *Mission of the University*:

In the thick of life's urgencies and its passions, the university must assert itself as a major "spiritual power," higher than the press, standing for serenity in the midst of frenzy, for seriousness and the grasp of intellect, in the face of frivolity and unashamed stupidity.[6]

Universities can be leaders, however, only when *they exemplify* high ideals and when their administrations and faculties not only endorse but exercise practices which reflect the values idealized by our society. In recent times institutions of higher learning, particularly the larger ones, have taken on the aura of big business corporations. Fund drives take precedence. Young professors quickly are indoctrinated into the knowing ways of their elders in "how to get ahead" and, consequently, they are often much too involved in the publish-or-perish conflict to be concerned properly with the responsibilities of teaching. A large percentage of undergraduate teaching is done by the young teacher who frequently views his duties in the classroom as a necessary evil while he establishes himself as an investigator, writer, or administrator. His goals often are complicated by the immediate need for promotion.

Another factor common to the average college teacher, young or old, is the impact of economic deprivation. This has serious implications for teaching values because the professor's standard of living may narrow his frame of reference and limit his aesthetic tastes. The teacher then becomes a rather slim value referent. Undoubtedly the most serious problem rests in the fact that, in general, college faculties support fully the view that responsibility of higher education is restricted chiefly to intellectual values and they are lukewarm or even opposed to assuming direct responsibility for student growth in other areas. Smith[7] cites five reasons why college faculties generally do not perceive the direct teaching of values as their responsibility: (1) According to the enlightenment view, education provides the individual with knowledge and reason; therefore it is assumed he will choose the good life. (2) All values are relative; therefore there are no universally valid standards by which to judge better from worse. (3) Maintenance of objectivity is a prerequisite to seeking truth; consequently concern for value may distort truth. (4) Division of labor is necessary in a complex society; therefore, the school is responsible for intellectual values while home and church care for moral values. (5) Respect for autonomy is necessary in higher education; thus students should be allowed to find their own means of gaining freedom. It is rather shocking to recognize that faculties have become so immersed in their separate disciplines that they have almost abdicated that which traditionally has been one of the primary responsibilities of education. The picture is not all black, however, and we can be assured that there will always be some faculty members who perceive the teaching of values as an important function.

In the last decade, there have been several notable studies of college teachers' concepts of what student values should be. Brown's statement summarizes these concepts:

Faculty see "ideal" students as having a high degree of intellectual power which is directed toward objects of intellectual interest in an independent manner and disciplined along integrative, penetrating and analytic lines. It is important, however, that the cognitive-intellectual aspects of the students' development not be one-sided so that qualities of friendliness, helpfulness, and cooperativeness not be lost nor the moral implications of one's intelligence be slighted.[8]

Opposed to this ideal, an observer of the American college scene, Christopher Jencks, pictures the following as actuality:

In talking with undergraduates in these . . . colleges I often got the impression that no faculty, no matter how ingenious, could overcome the students' impulses against taking books and ideas seriously. Such students did not seem to want to become involved in academic life, for they did not want to feel guilty about not completing assignments, much less about not inventing extra as-

signments for self-improvement. They wanted their college to be just like any other office, at which they would arrive at nine o'clock to put in eight hours of work for a decent wage of grades and course credits. And they wanted to leave at five, free men.[9]

This general picture of student attitude, though somewhat harsh, is reinforced by the results of four recent comprehensive studies of college students' values. Specifically, students conceive of education as serving a utilitarian purpose: learning how to get along with people and acquiring techniques necessary for success in society. Other characteristics observed in the current crop of students include the valuing of self-attainment to the exclusion of concern for others; the development of group dependence which permits rationalization of personal conduct and standards as necessary for achieving belongingness; and an almost total social and political indifference with an accompanying lack of responsibility. While professing religious beliefs and a need for believing, they do not feel strongly committed to these convictions; and although professing esteem for the traditional moral virtues of honesty, sincerity, and loyalty, they do not feel obligated to observe these standards when the opposite behavior seems socially acceptable.

The wide schism is the core of the problem faced by educators in their efforts to help students strengthen their resources and actions involving value judgments. In order to aid in the orientation of student values, the university must: (1) Strive to make the needs of the individual the prime referent of social behavior; (2) Demonstrate to the student the total role of the enlightened citizen; (3) Become a force in improving social conditions in the community, thus demonstrating a commitment to social responsibility; and (4) Observe honesty in all forms, thereby preventing bias from clouding judgments. If the university observed these four ideals it might well achieve the utopian function described by Frederick Mayer:

It is to create a new society in which rationality will prevail, in which beauty will become a way of life, in which science will be used constructively, in which virtue and knowledge will coincide, and in which creative ideas will make for human happiness.[10]

Guiding Value Development

The results of research fail to present a rosy picture regarding the values of entering college students or their susceptibility to change: 20 to 25 per cent reveal varying degrees of change in interest, attitude, and value orientation by the time of their graduation. Educators must look hopefully to this small symbol of success and increase their efforts to strengthen the value orientation of college students.

As discussed earlier, we know that the individual develops preferential ways of behaving which are identified with self and are central to his needs. The individual's identification of self is a primary factor in his ability to bind together the values derived from all of his experiences. As these experiences increase in number and become more complex, the individual is faced with conflicting values, such as intelligent, conscientious work will enable him to reach his goals but knowing the "right" people may be even more important; a liberal education is valuable but certain carefully chosen vocations will lead to "success." He is pressured from all sides to conform, yet "to get ahead," he is told, one must be an individual in every respect.

The average student enters college with a fair concept of his self-identity; he has begun to cope with value conflicts; and he is still influenced by parental values. The values derived from his cultural background are reinforced each time that he communicates with family and friends. Despite this deep entrenchment of values, freshmen reveal a great potential for change. Nevitt Sanford sums it up explicitly when he writes

. . .It is possible for a student to become after four years of college or less, relatively broad in outlook and open to new experience, independent and disciplined in his thinking, deeply committed to some productive activity, possessed of convictions based on understanding of the world and on his own integration of personality.[11]

The extent to which the student becomes the individual just described depends in large part upon the nature of the educational environment provided during his college years. This environment includes the perceived purposes of the college, the structure of student peer groups, curricular and extracurricular experiences, and the faculty. Let us examine the potential contributions of each of these in the guidance of student values.

We can picture the college or university as a big circle enveloping students, faculty, curricula, and the innumerable facets of higher education. To become something more than a catalogue, *the institution must stand for something.* One of the greatest factors in inducing change in college students is the climate of the institution. Some colleges revere superior intellectual endeavor, others stress world-mindedness, still others center on a sense of community responsibility.

The institution's well-defined model provides a general frame of reference that gives rise to a community of values developed and internalized by participants in the life of the college. This model in a sense also provides a level of expectancy that is mutually developed by the college and its students. It is well known that young people select a college because it idealizes something they desire. When this is the case, the students will reinforce the college model by demanding experiences commensurate with it and exhibiting behavior that demonstrates their willingness to identify with it. The young man who chooses Annapolis expects among other things to strengthen his sense of honor and personal integrity. The girl who chooses Sarah Lawrence anticipates hard work and independent study.

It is clear that each institution of higher education must not only have a well defined model, but also must not lack in expectancy of excellence in more than one direction. A model that is limited to the ideal of superior intellectual endeavor alone is no more sufficient than one which is constricted by the single label of athletic superiority. To become a potent factor in value development, the institution must furnish a model that is liberal in scope and filled with idealism in the sphere of desirable values for its students.

A second major factor is what Seth Arsenian refers to as a "person-centered environment rather than a mass-centered environment." Many institutions give rise to the feeling of mass education merely because of their physical environment which is necessitated by the size of the student enrollment. Large state universities are particularly conscious of this problem. Many of these large schools, fortunately, have found a measure of success in personalizing the education of masses. Although each high rise dormitory may house as many as two thousand students, campus architects have found ways to design living arrangements so that they produce a homelike atmosphere. The problems inherent in mass living provide value-laden experiences which, with wise guidance, can contribute to the value maturation of each student. The administration must utilize all available opportunities and create new ones to guide students in achieving greater personal responsibility for their behavior.

A campus climate that promotes student responsibility eventually will permeate even the most hidebound departments and impel faculties to *guide* students in making wise decisions. It cannot be assumed that because the student can read the catalogue he will become educated, that all he need do is meet the academic requisites stipulated therein. Faculty guidance is necessary to help students achieve personal autonomy.

And so we see that the college that is truly concerned with its responsibility to guide students in achieving sound values has many opportunities to set the stage for this moral awakening. These include a clearly identified model with well defined values cherished by the institution, a continuous effort to utilize a person-centered approach to all aspects of students' experiences, and encouragement of all students to become involved in a variety of issues requiring value judgment on their part. In assuming this vital role the institution consciously establishes ideals of adulthood, including (1) achievement of personal autonomy; (2) fulfillment of a human being's potentialities; and (3) sensitive recognition of social responsibilities.

Educators have long recognized the powerful influence exerted on an individual by his peers. This influence often presents a crucial area of interaction for the undergraduate who, like most of his acquaintances, has a need to establish independence from his parents and achieve adult status in this intermediate zone where he is considered as half child and half adult. Stretched out but not cut loose from his home influence, the freshman in particular seeks identification with those who will reinforce the interests and value system which he brought to college. The freshman's almost immediate identification with fellow students whose views are in harmony with his can make the task of value reorientation a more difficult one if these views are not consonant with the values or objectives of the college.

Increased student enrollments with their accompanying problems complicate the institution's efforts. Unless careful steps are initiated, the major influence of the home on the student is quickly supplanted by one or more groups of students to whom he is drawn. Living on campus should provide an ideal opportunity for students to discuss concepts taken from the classroom and to speculate about their implications for achieving the goals of a satisfactory life. Students, however, tend to separate the intellectual domain from their nonacademic campus life. Small colleges fortunately have been successful in their efforts to utilize peer-group influence in the integration of the intellectual with the social aspect of student life. Theodore Newcomb[12] lists three factors which he considers necessary if large colleges are to achieve the same degree of effectiveness: (1) Establish college units of no more than 300 to 400; (2) Construct living arrangements so that an overlap occurs with membership in a formal college unit; (3) Insure the quality of the student-faculty contact rather than emphasize its frequency.

The learning process includes the teacher, the learner, and the subject matter but these three are so closely interwoven that it is difficult to separate one from another. We shall attempt, nevertheless, to examine separately the curriculum and the teacher for the essentials conducive to the development of values. Curriculum as defined here refers to the environment and substance contained within a given course.

In his discussion of ways in which to free intelligence Gardner Murphy describes the teaching-learning situation as a process in which the teacher and the student mutually search for a "more meaningful understanding of themselves and their world." Such a learning environment is certainly the antithesis of the traditional dispensing of facts with little thought given to their utilization beyond memorization.

There are three basic factors that play an important role in the development of values in the context of the classroom: (1) Factual information; (2) Personal sensitivity to the use of knowledge; and (3) A capacity for critical analysis of conflicting issues requiring the use of knowledge. There is little question that the average student readily acquires the first factor. Achievement of the second and third require considerable intent, thought, and planning. A student may or may not arrive in a course with pre-established sensitivity to its focus. Certainly, however, the instructor has an opportunity and obligation not only to pique the student's interest but also to create in him an awareness of the implications of all that he learns.

Avoiding sole use of the lecture method is a first step in setting the stage for improving personal sensitivity to facts. Posing questions which require consideration of appropriate factual information in a social context of community, nation, and world becomes an important second step. Students should be encouraged to raise questions in the process of searching for the application of specific knowledge to societal use. Through this process they may achieve a perceptiveness of their world which aids in developing personal sensitivity. A third step is an extension of the second. Topics of papers that are to be prepared can be so selected and examinations can be so constructed that the student's use of knowledge is extended beyond mere recall. Heightened interest and enthusiasm by the student for the subject matter often results in an intellectual concomitant that evolves from efforts to increase personal sensitivity to knowledge.

Efforts to increase the student's personal sensitivity result in part in improving his ability to think. Seeking answers to his questions about the practical use of information requires a student to exercise his ability to examine issues carefully. Because values are more likely to develop from matters which are of central concern, it behooves the instructor to guide the selection of issues to those which are perceived by the students as important. This process of selection also affords the instructor opportunities to include within the range of issues some which are related to the model of the institution, thus bridging the gap between the intellectual aspect of the classroom and the campus life of the student. If the course is to foster development of personal values then the prime requisite of any issue selected for analysis is the degree of conflict it creates within each student.

When presenting an issue the instructor must be prepared to assist the students in: (1) Identifying the focus of the question, (2) Providing general factual information related to it, (3) Identifying preliminary solutions, (4) Pinpointing conflicts inherent in each solution, (5) Ascertaining further knowledge specifically related to existing conflicts, and (6) Applying principles of personal value commitment in reaching a tentative final solution. All of the foregoing steps are necessary in the use of critical thinking, a process discussed in another chapter. Suffice it to note here that this approach not only guides the student toward increased concern for human issues, but also helps him to understand his personal responsibility for the use of knowledge. He is then able to derive principles that guide him in reaching a solution consonant with the ideals of the society in which he lives.

The teacher is seldom as effective in inducing value change in a student as one might expect. When value orientation does occur, however, it usually does so in situations involving student-faculty interaction. Often a value expressed by a teacher will fall, as Gordon Allport describes it, "on the student's present growing edge." Frequently young people must believe in someone else's ideas before they can believe in their own. The student may incorporate the teacher as his model for identification. In doing so, he assumes the expressed values of the teacher. Faced with this appalling responsibility, institutions of higher education can ill afford to select faculty who perceive their contribution to be identified solely with disseminating the facts of a single discipline.

Let us make the assumption that all college teachers wish to share in shaping their students' value judgments. What is it that marks the difference in this respect between the memorable professor and the one soon forgotten? A dedication to the belief that he can and will make an impact on his students is surely the starting point. This alone will insure thoughtful planning.

A second requisite of the effective teacher is a well-defined personal value commitment. All of the major value studies to date indicate that the greatest degree of value change occurs in situations in which teachers express firm value commitments. This does not imply that the classroom should become a ground for personal indoctrination. It means simply that faculty must take advantage of opportunities to express values as they are *appropriately* related to the subject matter under discussion. This then opens the door for further discussion which permits the student to recognize that the values expressed by his professor evolved from a process of logical thought rather than from quick decision or rationalization. Frequent observations of this practice help students realize the importance of committing themselves intelligently to a sound viewpoint.

A warmth of personality is a third factor that distinguishes the effective teacher from the ineffective one in developing values. It is impossible to estimate the effect on college students of the warm, loving, mature adult who looks beyond his own aspirations in his concern for the maturity development of his students. Students know that such a teacher *cares* what happens to them. These are not teachers who become overly involved in the lives of their students, but individuals marked by maturity and objectivity in their approach to teaching who give full release to their enthusiasm for their subject matter and their fellow-learner. Their patience and acceptance of students as persons with ideas often bear fruit with even the most cynical. Frequently it is this attitude of the teacher that creates a climate that frees students to see the instructor's values through his teaching demeanor, that permits them to challenge ideas, and leads them to the use of values in seeking solutions to academic and personal conflicts.

Personality Development: Growth in Knowledge

Earl V. Pullias

Teaching as described in this book is intimately related to personality. Crucial to all effective teaching is the personality of the teacher, for in the learning-teaching situation, in an important sense, what is to be learned is mediated through the teacher's personality.

If one tries to understand the power of the world's greatest teachers, he is steadily led toward the conclusion that life and meaning were given to their teaching by a special quality of their personalities. These personalities are greatly varied, but a common thread seems to run through all examples of powerful teaching: that to be considered or learned, mediated through the teacher, becomes alive and meaningful in a special way and reaches the learner as vital, direct experience. This quality is manifested by Socrates, Hillel, Abelard, Mark Hopkins, William James, William Rainey Harper, Woodrow Wilson, Frederick Jackson Turner, Louis Agassiz, Anne Sullivan Macy, Alfred North Whitehead, Mahatma Gandhi, and a multitude of other less celebrated but perhaps equally great teachers. The essence of the teaching art lies in the character of the person.

One purpose of teaching is to influence the personality development of students. Teaching in its best sense thus aims to assist in the unfolding of the learner towards the fullest development of his potential as a self. Prolonged and intimate interaction between more mature learners (called teachers) and less mature learners (called students) at many levels of interest and concern is very nearly the core of the teaching-learning process. If this process goes on in the optimum climate of learning, remarkable things can happen to both teacher and taught.

But there is great risk to the personalities of both the teacher and the student in the formal educative process. Let us examine the situation from the standpoint of the teacher.

There is a serious occupational hazard in teaching. Every person who enters teaching as a profession must face the danger of serious personality damage through his work. Some students of this problem (George Williams in *Some of My Best Friends Are Professors*, for example) conclude that many persons choose teaching because of basic personality defects and inadequacies, and that the strains of teaching tend merely to magnify these tendencies. Others feel that the major cause of the personality type often considered typical of the teacher is the very special strains which accompany teaching, together with undesirable mental and physical health practices. An analysis from this angle can be found in Arthur Jersild's *When Teachers Face Themselves*.[1]

Whatever the basic cause, it seems to be clear that teachers tend to develop two widely divergent types of personality and character as a result of prolonged teaching. I am aware that there is no scientific proof of this bimodal distribution of teacher personality, but long experience with and observation of teachers lead me to suggest this situation as a hypothesis. Perhaps, in time, research will throw further light on the problem.

One group of teachers under the special stresses and demands that accompany teaching develop markedly less desirable traits with increased experience. In these cases, teaching, instead of being a means to positive personality development or to full self-actualization (to use A. H. Maslow's phrase), produces progressive personality damage. As these teachers grow older they come more and more to typify the common stereotype of the school teacher: harassed, irritable, insecure, defensive, punitive, opinionated, garrulous, condescending, lonely, infantile. Development of such personality is a professional hazard of the first magnitude.

No one is immune to this danger. I speak as a teacher of more than thirty years' experience who loves and respects the great profession of teaching. To refuse to see what happens to a very large proportion of teachers at all levels is not to be loyal to the profession nor to serve it best. If teachers, especially college teachers, could see themselves as they often are and as others see them, this self-understanding might be an important step toward finding the cause and changing the results.

Often when this point is discussed, defensive teachers urge that the negative picture of the teacher is an old stereotype, stemming from the days of the bespectacled, lonely spinster with fierce countenance and severe hairdo, bound by Puritan habits, or the awkward, fear-ridden man for whom teaching was the last resort for a livelihood. And, it is urged, none of these things is true of the modern teacher.

The problem is infinitely deeper. Surface sophistication manifested in various frenetic attempts to be "free" and like "everyone else" is no evidence of wholesome personality. A distorted personality may manifest itself in the classroom, in faculty activities, and in the wider community, in those who dress in the latest fashion, who have families, who sport the latest hairdo or haircut, who travel, who pride themselves in being "unbound" in personal habits and beliefs. In fact, it seems to me that the most unattractive defenses against the great demands of the teacher's life often appear under a heavy layer of "modern" sophistication. The point is that the problem presented here is not solved by saying that the teacher of today is accepted in the most up-to-date society. Rather we must look squarely at what we all too often are and how we behave.

Teaching does not always damage or distort personality. There is the other group of teachers (let us hope increasing in numbers) who are continuously enriched by their teaching experience. Each year of teaching makes their personalities more desired and more desirable. For reasons not yet altogether clear, the stresses and special demands of the life of a teacher are the means of growth. As these teachers grow older (and even old) they come to typify the teacher at his best: kindly, stimulating, inquiring, mature, thoughtful, objective, confident, joyful, sincere, creative. Such personality is a professional satisfaction and reward of the first magnitude.

These men and women are in the beloved and honored tradition of the great teachers of mankind in all the phases of man's effort at civilization on this planet. They usually have not been well rewarded materially. Often they have felt it necessary to avoid material affluence in order to be free, for perhaps above everything a teacher must be free. Many societies have revered the teacher, but perhaps the richest traditions are those of the Hebrew people and some nations of the Orient.

For the teacher, teaching thus may be either a way to personality ruin or to personality enrichment and fulfillment. To me it is as if there were a divide, as on a roof or on land. If the personality is slanted in one way, the blows and demands which come upon it carry it farther and farther in an undesirable direction. If the same or almost the same circumstances come upon a personality slanted in another direction, the very obstacles and demands become a means of carrying it to richer and fuller realization.

Every student of the psychology of personality would like to know the major causes for the difference between these two groups. Of course, this question does not apply only to teachers, for all people are either enriched or impoverished by the living of life. I believe however that teachers are more subject to the working of the principle (that the hammer blows of life produce the extremes of desirable and undesirable personality) than most other groups because of the very special demands of teaching.

The nature of these demands and their particular threat to personality are not fully understood. The key to the matter may be found in the emotional strain that comes from continuous interaction with numerous and varied personalities in a fluid relation that is characterized by strongly ambivalent feelings and by inescapable responsibility. Whatever the cause, everyone who has taught surely knows that the emotional, physical, and intellectual strain is very great. Stated in another and more positive way, the experiences involved in teaching tend to be intimate, direct, intense, and unpredictable.

It becomes clear then that if these experiences or interactions are received constructively or wisely, the personality will be remarkably enriched and stimulated to growth. If, for any of a variety of reasons, they are received negatively or unwisely, the personality must develop defenses or ways of reacting that make the demands bearable. These negative defensive reactions become harmful and unattractive personality traits often associated with the teacher stereotype.

But the important problem for us as teachers is what seems to make the difference and what can be done about it. Evidently the problem is very complex. The varied literature on mental hygiene which has grown up in the last fifty years bears on this issue. In my judgment, the most promising and helpful recent work is that reported by A. H. Maslow in *Motivation and Personality*,[2] and in his later book, *Toward a Psychology of Being*.[3] His study and analysis of the healthy or whole personality as opposed to the more classical emphasis upon the pathological, as a means to self-understanding, have great value for the teacher interested in developing personality through teaching.

Because of the complexity of the problems of personality healing and growth, it is risky to give brief and relatively simple answers to the question of what makes the difference between the teacher who is damaged by teaching and the one who is healed and enriched by it. Nevertheless I wish to venture a few simple and practical suggestions. The basic concept and a sketch of the suggestions were mentioned at the end of Chapter 4. A partial filling in of that sketch in this connection may help teachers in their search for approaches to teaching that will not only safeguard the personality from the dangers inherent in a career in taeching, but which will enable them to use the severe and special demands of teaching as a means to the fullest personality development.

The key, I believe, is continuous growth. In every person there is a deep and urgent need to come to rest, to find the answer, to arrive, to culminate the struggle. Perhaps it was this longing in its essence that Freud was suggesting in the "death instinct." Be that as it may, it seems that individuals and the varied groups of individuals which compose organized society live under the illusion that just over the brow of this next hill the top will be reached, or at least a top where gains can be consolidated, interests can be hedged in and shored up, and the desperate quality can go out of struggle.

This desire for culmination, for rest, for final balance, is so great that both individuals and groups strive to produce the reality by pretending to themselves and others that they have arrived. If the pretense is strong enough, growth stops and in a deep sense the death need begins to be satisfied, for death sets in whenever growth ceases. Such evidence as is available suggests that in the universe as we know it there is no point of equilibrium or balance; there is progressive unfolding and differentiation which we call growth, or there is deterioration in the direction of the full disintegration of death.

If this is a truth, it is one of the big truths with almost limitless implications for the management of human life. In relation to our problem of "through teaching to personality development" it simply means that the teacher either is growing toward the full actualization of himself or he is dying. This sort of death process is accompanied by all the painful psychological defenses which our generation has read so much about. The teacher who ceases to grow, as a matter of self-defense in an attempt to make life bearable, fights a rear guard action against deterioration. The unattractive traits developed by so many teachers are the practical manifestation of this struggle against the most frightening of all threats: the frustration of unfulfilled potential and the loss of such integrity of self as may have been achieved.

The growth side of the picture is as bright as the deterioration side is dark. There is a strong persistent need for all human beings to realize their full potential. Life can be made up primarily of the deep satisfactions of a growth process which leads steadily to the full realization of the self. For such persons, the circumstances of life varying from joy to sorrow, from triumph to failure, from pleasure to great suffering, become grist for the mill of this growth that leads to a fuller and fuller life. This is an ideal, a goal, that is rarely reached in individual lives, but the potential exists and the potential seems to produce a longing for its fulfillment.

The working teacher who wishes to avoid the evil of crystal-lization and consequent deterioration and to achieve that meas-ure of growing maturity which is the only meaningful protection of personality would like to have some practical help. What does this growth involve and how can it be encouraged? As mentioned in an earlier chapter, full development which sustains and con-tinuously re-creates life in the human personality is constituted of growth in *knowledge* and growth in *being*.

Thus the teacher who would achieve the fullest personality growth through teaching must find the means in these two phases of the self. A brief analysis of each may be helpful.

To be alive in any genuine sense is to be learning. The odyssey which leads to ever-widening areas of knowing is lifelong. It seems to be in the very nature of man to extend the self through a fuller comprehension of the nature of things. Gardner Murphy expresses this thought convincingly in *Freeing Intelligence Through Teaching*.[4] This need to know and to understand (which is an aspect of knowing) is strongest when life is strongest, i.e., in childhood and youth, and decreases only under the pressure of fear, routine, and other life-inhibiting forces. Let us examine briefly five aspects of this growth in knowing which are essential to the life of the personality.

1. The self. Of all the doctrines of religion and philosophy there are few more important to health of personality than the ancient Delphic admonition, "Know thyself." The self is the basic instrument with which life is lived. To be ignorant of either strengths or weaknesses of that instrument is to invite trouble or even disaster.

No one can hope to acquire full understanding of the vast un-charted land which is a human self, but everyone can enter upon the path to self-knowledge. Every teacher should set increasing self-knowledge as a prime goal of his personal and professional life. The study can be divided in many ways for convenience in observation. For example, one who must by the nature of his work be under considerable physical and psychological tensions needs to have a good knowledge of his body. Relatively simple information about energy supply and renewal, optimum diet, fatigue level, stress tolerance, exercise need and other such body peculiarities may enable the teacher to use his body more effectively. Fatigue narrows perspective and distorts perception and judgment. It seems that many of the foolish things teachers do are a direct or indirect result of overfatigue. And it may be that lack of imagination and general "dead-headedness" in teaching are due in a great measure to a low energy level. Many teachers have found the work of the Canadian physician, Hans Selye, helpful in understanding and dealing with stress.[5]

Equally important is a growing knowledge of what is usually termed the mind. What are its innate or acquired tender spots? Under what conditions, at what rate, and on what type of tasks does it perform best? What are its major natural or at least deeply embedded interests or concerns? How much stress can this particular mind take before it begins to produce protective symptoms? Most important of all, what are this mind's special qualities or abilities that have distinctive promise for cultivation?

These are merely a few of the questions that the seeker for self-knowledge asks and attempts to answer about his individual mind: its nature, potential, limits, weaknesses, and strengths. At its best, this instrument is one of the remarkable phenomena in a universe of complex and remarkable things. Distorted by malfunction or limited by failure in normal growth, the mind presents an example of extreme ineffectiveness and unattractiveness. The typical person takes his mind for granted, leaving great areas of it fallow, and using it badly. Too much concern might become morbid, but to understand something of the delicate complexity of a fine machine or organism is not necessarily to become pathologically preoccupied about its care.

The third large phase of the self is so complex and unavailable for study through the methods to which we are accustomed that there is a hesitancy to speak about the spirit of man. Yet the witness of the most thoughtful men of every age is that the quality called spirit is the central essence of man as man. The evidence is strong that he denies or negates this part of himself at great peril. Man is a biological organism with very special mental equipment, but when either as an individual or in social organizations he is only that, he rapidly loses his distinctively human qualities and becomes an ineffective and unattractive animal. The

distortion of human personality which results from the high development of physical and mental abilities and the neglect of
spiritual potential produces a horrible being.

This subject is clearly very complex. It will suffice to suggest
here that if a teacher hopes to understand his full self,
he should free himself as rapidly as possible from childishly negative attitudes (often rooted in early unwise religious training)
toward problems of the spirit of man which so frequently have
caused a thin sophisticated blindness in modern man, and set
himself to a study of this most intriguing part of himself. I
should like to suggest three books that many students have found
helpful: Franz Winkler's *Man: The Bridge Between Two Worlds*[6]
(the approach of a psychiatrist); Aldous Huxley's *The Perennial
Philosophy*[7] (a more philosophic and mystical view); and Paul
Tillich's *The Dynamics of Faith*[8] (a theological view).

In the search for growth in the understanding of self, the complex human personality should not be broken into segments except perhaps for convenience in study. The self, particularly the
healthy self, is a whole. The teacher is urged to seek understanding, by all available means, of this entity which determines the
quality and meaning of a human life.

2. Nature of man. Man is a social animal, as Aristotle observed long ago. The wide implications of this fact still are being
examined through the various disciplines that make man as individual and as organization or institution the center of their study.
One thinks especially of anthropology, psychology, and sociology;
but economics, political science, biology, history, literature cannot be omitted. A great proportion of man's intellectual effort
has gone into the study of himself and his institutions.

The teacher, of course, cannot hope to become expert in all
these areas. He need not do so. But the teacher's effectiveness
depends much upon his understanding of man: his achievements,
foibles, powers, institutions. Neglect to grow in this intriguing
area of knowledge is not only to court failure in one's work but,
equally important, is to cut oneself off from one of life's greatest
pleasures.

I am tempted to offer suggestions for reading, observation, and
record keeping that have been helpful for some who are seeking

means of growth toward the deeper understanding of other selves. Perhaps it is better that each seek his own most satisfying and rewarding avenues. Certainly the search should not be limited to formal study through reading and thought about the behavior and achievements of man in general.

A teacher's life by its very nature is in constant relation with a wide variety of people. A habit of careful observation, with some recording and analysis, contributes greatly to understanding of others. That is, a teacher lives in the best of all psychological and sociological laboratories. Viewed in one way, these close and continuous relations with people are irritating and boring—a situation to be borne with fortitude and escaped as soon as possible; but approached differently, they are a rich and abiding source of learning. It seems strange that a person would feel the need to go away to some special place to study the behavior of people when every classroom, every college or university as a community is at hand for study.

Whatever the means used, the goal suggested is a steadily enlarging knowledge of other selves, as individuals and as groups.

3. The achievements of man. There is much that is dark and ugly about man's experience on this planet. He seems to learn extremely slowly, and in some areas almost not at all, except over long periods. Professor Crane Brinton in the first chapter of the significant book *Ideas and Men*[9] classifies man's knowledge and achievement into the "cumulative" (scientific knowledge and application which apparently accumulates steadily over the historical period) and "non-cumulative" (art, poetry, ethics, etc. which reveal little if any progression over long periods).

However man's experience during the historical period of approximately five thousand years may be viewed, his achievements have been great. His strangely restless spirit never ceases to probe, to search, to build, to invent, to discover. More than two thousand years ago the poet Sophocles spoke of the powers and achievements of man in this way:

Many a wonder lives and moves, but the wonder of all is man,
. . .Wise utterance and wind-swift thought, and city-moulding mind,

. . . Inventive beyond wildest hope, endowed with boundless skill.[10]

Shakespeare expressed the same estimate of potential:

What a piece of work is man! How noble in reason! how infinite in faculties! in form and moving, how express and admirable! in action, how like an angel! in apprehension, how like a god! the beauty of the world! the paragon of animals!

Surely all of us in this culture are acquainted with the Psalmist's words:

What is man, that thou art mindful of him? . . . For thou hast made him a little lower than the angels, and hast crowned him with glory and honour. Thou madest him to have dominion over the works of thy hands; thou hast put all things under his feet.

A chief function of the teacher is to bring each rising generation into appreciative and imaginative relation with the varied achievements of man. It is the teacher's task to guide the young into a journey of exploration that will acquaint them in some measure at least with the heritage of mankind in thought and deed. It is true that the teacher's immediate responsibility usually will be limited to a small area of this heritage, but in view of the very close relationship among all phases of knowledge and achievement a particular subject can be greatly enriched if the teacher can place it in the framework of all of man's knowledge.

A constantly growing knowledge of the achievements of man has an even greater value for the teacher in its effect on him as a person. Through breadth of experience the teacher overcomes a dangerous tendency to overspecialize. Further, he may be able to rise above the narrow provincialism of time, nationality, race, culture or civilization. He comes to be a genuine citizen of the world, a worthy member of the human race, and thus gradually achieves the freedom of mind and tolerance of spirit which accompany growth toward wisdom.

The teacher freed of tribal and other fetters draws freely from all peoples of all times and places. His life is given breadth, depth, and joy as he shares freely in the efforts and achievements of the human race. In a sense, only through this wide experience can man become genuinely man, i.e., man at his best. There is nothing mystical or sentimental implied here. The very practical suggestion is that the teacher grow in knowledge of the magnificent achievements of man: art, literature, science, architecture, government, religion, law, music—the list is long, and ever grows longer.

I am aware that this is an age of specialization—a time when one cannot know even a narrow area well. Practical success seems to depend on a limited and constantly narrowing specialization. This situation with its threatening consequences offers a major support to the plea for breadth in the teachers, especially the college teachers, of our time. Growth in knowledge of the wide achievements of man will make the teacher a better teacher and a better person.

4. Nature and her processes. Man is, of course, an intimate part of the natural world. In spite of his relatively great achievements, he is actually a very small part of the mammoth scheme of nature. In the course of history man has often succumbed to the temptation to forget his smallness and his limitations, and has developed what might be called a "cosmic irreverence." It is good to take proper pride in significant achievement; it is dangerous to forget limitations. Such forgetting may lead man to engage in what the Greeks called *hubris* (a prideful, irresponsible, self-centered drive for power) which is followed by *nemesis* (the deterioration and eventual destruction consequent upon unbalanced arrogant striving).

Modern man seems to be in danger of such arrogance. Often he speaks of conquering Nature when he might better speak of understanding and cooperating with her. Man's current space achievements are significant, but they need to be put in proper perspective by a meditative look into a clear night sky, or perhaps better by a view now and then through a great telescope. The point is that nature is vast and unspeakably complex both as macrocosm and microcosm.

Reverence for nature and her processes does not suggest fear, superstition, or ignorance. The teacher who seeks the best personality development will make a lifetime study, at least as an amateur, of the natural world. Such study not only enriches the teacher's knowledge, but can be a great source of pleasure even into old age. Wherever such a teacher is or goes he is in the midst of phenomena and processes that are a boundless means of learning. It is a self-engendered curse to walk blind, deaf, and without feeling through the wonders of the natural world. No teacher even in a great modern city should so curse himself.

Only one other word can be said here about growth in knowledge of the natural world. For many years a strong belief has been growing in my mind that man long cut off from nature or improperly related to her becomes distorted and tends to grow sick, although there is no proof for that belief. Whatever the truth may be, many seekers for effectiveness in life have found regular, interested, and respectful contact with natural things both healing and growth-producing.

5. One's subject or special area of competence. In another section of the book the relation between excellence in teaching and the mastery of a special area of knowledge was emphasized. The same point has wider implications in this connection. The teacher who seeks the fullest self-actualization or the best in personality development will find that expert knowledge of a limited area of human experience (called a subject) will be very helpful.

In truth, there is no such thing as full mastery of even the most limited area of knowledge. All things are so interrelated that a *full* knowledge of even the smallest area (even Tennyson's "flower in a crannied wall") would mean a knowledge of all things.

Yet the idea of "mastery" of one's subject is a valuable one. We all know it is used in a relative sense. One can and should have a relative mastery of his subject at certain levels. Thus he will know more of it than most of those who are learners with him as students, and probably more than most other people. Such knowledge will give him confidence and a precious freedom of imagination.

However, where one is, as Lowell suggested, is not nearly so important as the direction one is traveling. That is, what one knows about his subject may be important, but of greater importance is constant *growth* in the knowledge of the area of one's special competence. By this means, depth is added to the dimension of breadth previously emphasized. This steady increase in depth in a single area gives special life and meaning to the whole spectrum of growth in knowledge so vital to the personality development of the teacher.

All these phases of growth in knowledge of self, of other selves, of man's achievement, of the natural world, and of one's special area of competence are a means toward the development of that degree of maturity which is the only effective guarantee that the person will be enriched by the experiences of life—even the special demands of a teacher's life. It should be clear that the absolute amount of knowledge is probably not very important—at best it is very little—but continuous growth in knowledge is the crucial matter.

Personality Development: Growth in Being

Earl V. Pullias

Growth in knowledge, which we have discussed somewhat in the foregoing chapter, cannot be separated from growth in being, for both growth and the self that grows are basically a whole. What one knows affects the quality of one's being; and also what one is influences the nature and quality of one's knowing and knowledge. Further, overt behavior is a manifestation of knowledge and being, and at the same time constantly molds both of them. Thus the intricate web of life is constituted of what one knows and is learning, of what one is and is becoming, and of what one does and is planning.

It is true that one may be well supplied in live, meaningful knowledge and not achieve optimum growth in being or becoming. Hence it may be helpful to suggest a few avenues of growth in being. The hope is that, as teachers, what we are will not contradict what we know and what we say, but will support our verbal professions. More important, growth in being is a crucial means to the quality of personality that is enriched by the demands of teaching.

1. Sensitivity. Quality of being is indicated in large measure by breadth and depth of sensitivity. There is a kind of sensitivity involved in knowing, but here we are concerned with an aspect of personality which permeates the whole self and has strong conative, cognitive, and affective tones. It manifests itself in numerous ways.

John Donne expressed one aspect of this sensitivity when, at the end of his famous words about man's relatedness, he said, ". . . and therefore never send to know for whom the bell tolls; it tolls for thee." This is an example of one's feelings reaching out to all everywhere who experience death. The principle holds with equal force in other phases of existence, including triumph and joy. In theory, the self extends to wider and wider reaches until it tends to partake of all experience, and in this sense partakes of the nature of the Infinite.

There is another phase of sensitivity which relates perhaps more apparently to personality growth and maturity. The widely sensitive person perceives with increasing rapidity the meaning of situations involving things or people. Technically speaking, he is able to assess the factors in a situation with a minimum of cues. Or put more practically, he does not have to know all the details in order to grasp the problem as a whole. Perhaps this sensitivity is manifested most meaningfully in a teacher in his ability to put himself in the place of others, and thus perceive their feelings.

Growth in sensitivity greatly strengthens and enriches the self, but there is latent danger here, against which a warning should be given. Sensitivity must be balanced by other qualities of knowing and being or the personality may find itself with a load it cannot carry. Man is finite and cannot bear an infinite burden. It is true that every hungry child in the world is in reality my child, but a high level of maturity is required if that type of sensitivity is to be carried wisely. The young poet Edna St. Vincent Millay in "Renascence" expressed the awful burden in these lines:

> *No hurt I did not feel, no death*
> *That was not mine; mine each last breath*
> *That, crying, met an answering cry,*
> *From the compassion that was I.*[1]

She found it a burden sufficient to crush the heart until she had moved upward by a new birth. As the teacher grows in sensitivity, he grows in other dimensions of personality, and is not only able to bear this breadth of feeling but feels himself only part man without it.

Teachers who have the desire and courage to plunge deeper into the intriguing problem of the relation between the growing self and the nonself, and the effect of that relation on personality health, will find a brilliant analysis by the novelist Richard Hughes in chapters 26-28 of *The Fox in the Attic*.[2] This author presents excellent psychological insights, particularly on the dangers of the irresponsible overextension of the self, in the clear and interesting language of a great novelist.

2. Interest and curiosity. In her sensitive book, *The Journey*,[3] Lillian Smith asks the question, "What is this stubborn thing in man that keeps him forever picking the lock of time?" It seems to be in his basic nature to do so. We call this part of his complex nature interest and curiosity.

Much of man's probing and searching has been in an attempt to solve practical problems. Much more of the unceasing search is to try to satisfy his insatiable need to explore, to experience, to understand. These qualities are a part of the essence of man, of what keeps him alive and growing as man. When routine, fear, illness, or habit destroys interest and curiosity, the vibrant quality of life tends to go out of the person.

The teacher who desires to continue growing and hence actualize his personality through teaching cultivates the roots of wide interests and restless curiosity. Like the most "alive" people who have lived, he spends his "time in nothing else, but either to tell, or to hear some new thing." But interest is a greater joy and profit than curiosity. To see every object and event in life with the fresh attention of a wholesome child is to have at hand an inexhaustible source of mental stimulation.

Narrowed interests mean a narrowed self. The overnarrowed self, however expert it may be in a limited field (a great danger to the college teacher), will fulfill the prophecy of the poet: "And he whose soul is flat—the sky will cave in on him by and by."[1]

Fortunately, interest and curiosity are such positive forces in personality that they need a minimum of cultivation; usually they need only to be protected and given a chance to express themselves. But the wise teacher will be alert to the symptoms of dying interest, will strive to avoid undue fatigue, and will seek varied and new experiences to whet interest and nourish curiosity. New places, different problems, new associates, varied challenges (even if self-set) help to keep interest alive.

The point of these observations is that interest and curiosity are both a symptom and a cause of life and growth in the working teacher. It is balanced growth that enables the teacher to take the demands of life in a way that brings continuing personality development.

3. Love. This great word (one is tempted to say this greatest of words) has been so loosely and badly used that many are hesitant to use it, or use it largely cynically. I find that many college teachers and other advanced graduate students are embarrassed when love is discussed. They seem to be afraid of the subject, yet evidently many in our world are love-starved and would profit from a frank expression of their need.

Perhaps nearly all of us have been wounded more or less deeply in our love relations. This fact may not be the fault of anyone or even of the culture (although doubtless grievous individual and cultural mistakes are made), but may arise from the extremely complex nature of love in all its myriad expressions. Yet I am convinced that there is a common essence in every manifestation of love, both giving and receiving.

In love we come to, or at least near, the ultimate in all the phases of existence: physical, mental, and spiritual. What is the relation between the love of the professional prostitute and that of the service-centered saint? Of the self-sacrificing mother and the adolescent afire with first physical infatuation? Of the friend for friend, and the seasoned husband and wife? Of course, I do not know. But the relation is there, and the implications are profound for human life. It may be that running through all of love is the losing of self and the concerns of self in a concern for the welfare and happiness of another. However misguided this quality may be, within it, if it is genuine, lie healing and creativity. Teachers interested in pursuing this point may find the introduction to *Saviors of God*,[4] by the Greek poet, Nikos Kazantzakis, stimulating.

The nature and meaning of love have been a major concern of the best minds of mankind from Plato's justly famous "Symposium" and Paul the Apostle's Corinthian poem to the insightful analysis of C. S. Lewis or the modern psychiatrists. It is not necessary to fathom this thought and analysis to conclude that the ability to give and receive love is crucial to personality health and growth. The evidence from every source available, including the best in psychological theory and research, supports this conclusion. Indeed it seems true that man must love and be loved or perish.

The teacher should know that there are many kinds of love to be given and received. There is a wide variety of human temperaments which seem to deal with love in different ways. Our present knowledge about this problem is sketchy, and the problem is of great complexity. Thus there is serious danger of false, harmful generalizations. For example, many single teachers have been advised by self-styled experts that they cannot be wholesome and well without the giving and receiving of physical love, and have been urged to seek such experience without regard to other needs of the personality. Such irresponsible advice acted upon usually compounds the original problem. Many types of temperament seem to be able to live a full creative life without certain manifestations of love. Even the deep need for love can be satisfied wisely only in terms of the values held by the whole self. To violate this principle is to court disaster.

Be that as it may, the teacher who would grow in love—the ability to give and receive self-forgetting concern—must seek and find healthy and growth-producing love expressions. The particular manifestations differ with individual temperament and are as varied as life itself. Each growing teacher will seek appropriate experiences of love, but he will seek them as the pearl of great price.

4. Self-determination. It is reported that the last words of Buddha to his disciples were that they must make their own environment. In an important sense, no man is truly free until he can produce his own environment whatever his apparent circumstances may be. Slavery to changing conditions tends to enslave all of life. A person so dependent may lose self-respect unless he is flattered or is overtly successful; he may be overwhelmed with fear or beside himself with pride at the loss or gain of economic

security or affluence; he may lose courage when things go against him.

Few things are more important to the growth toward maturity which we as teachers are seeking to understand, and perhaps in a measure achieve, than self-determination. Growth in this quality means an increasing ability to feel and behave in terms of resources which are within the self. These resources are always available, and strengthened and guided by them, the individual's thought and behavior are not subject to every chance change of fate. His standards and the strength to live by them come more and more to be in himself, and hence ever present and dependable.

A few illustrations may make the principle of self-determination clearer. The maturity of a class is indicated by the extent that external events influence its behavior. A slight change in the room, such as a simple accident or the appearance of an animal often will produce disorder in a group of less mature children. As they grow the controls of their behavior become internalized and if they are reasonably healthy emotionally, they will be less and less influenced by external events. The more mature class will behave about the same whether or not the teacher is present or the environmental circumstances favorable. The reactions of its members are not primarily determined by external conditions but by principle that centers in the self.

The behavior of many adults is guided chiefly by external requirements. They follow regulations in regard to traffic or litter or business ethics if they feel there is a likelihood they will be seen or in some way brought to account for the violations. Others reach that level of maturity where the standards for their actions are little or not at all dependent upon sanctions from without, but rest upon a flexible, growing body of principle—essentially a philosophy of life—that is based in truth as they are able to perceive it.

One other example closely related to the teaching-learning process will suffice. A discouragingly large number of students come, through their formal education, to conceive of learning primarily as meeting the requirements set by the teacher. This is the "lesson-learning attitude" referred to earlier which is so destructive of genuine learning. Teachers may develop the same attitude when caught in the whirl of too much "publish or perish" or other similar pressure. The key to understanding this attitude in oneself or others is to see that the activity involved has lost its meaning or significance except as a means of satisfying an external authority or surmounting what seems to be an artificial hurdle. The person involved is not self-determined and, to the degree that he is not, is essentially a slave.

Most important of all, the self-determined person is free in one of the most meaningful senses of that great concept. He is free from the vexing caprice of varied and rapidly changing circumstances. He is able to view failure or success, praise or blame, flattery or abuse, with equal poise because he has developed an increasingly stable and dependable process by which to judge the reality of the situation. Such freedom is in no sense irresponsible, or determined by impulse or personal whim. It is controlled and guided by the limits of truth or reality and such wisdom as the person has been able to acquire, but the crucial point is that the limits are self-accepted and self-imposed in the case of the self-determined person. Those who wish to pursue this point further may read Edith Hamilton's *Echo of Greece*,[5] particularly the first chapter.

The teacher who desires to find the fullest development of personality for himself and his students through teaching will strive to grow in self-determination. The poise and flexible stability thus achieved can do much to make teaching a growth-producing experience.

5. Humility. Does one dare speak of humility in a world which is very nearly mad for power, prestige, honor? I think so. The truth, the nature of things, is not changed by any particular madness that arises at a particular place or time. It may be that humility is not the best word to use, for its deepest meanings have been lost or distorted by caricatures of genuine humility. Perhaps reverence or awe in the presence of the Universe comes nearer to the meaning we seek. Professor Whitehead says: "And the foundation of reverence is this perception, that the present holds within itself the complete sum of existence, backwards and forwards, that whole amplitude of time, which is eternity."[6]

Two other great men of this age, Albert Einstein and Albert Schweitzer, have given emphasis to this point in both word and manner of life.

Humility as used here is the opposite of an overwhelming pride. It helps one to understand his proper place in the larger scheme of things. Such humility of mind is the foundation of respect for other people and their varying abilities. It is a stimulation and support to growing interest and curiosity: the very heart of the lifelong learning attitude. The teacher who is achieving this reverence is recognized by students and fellow-teachers as another learner in life's unending school. Few traits open up the gates of continuous and cooperative learning more effectively than a genuine spirit of humble reverence before what is to be learned and the process of learning.

This spirit should not be confused with lack of confidence, self-effacement, or fear. These things are often overt manifestations of unrequited pride or distorted self-centeredness. Genuine humility or reverence is crucial to the most creative self-confidence. I believe no one would consider Albert Einstein or Helen Keller or Abraham Lincoln either proud or groveling; rather they had the incomparable strength of genuine humility and the wholesome awe that accompanies it.

What a relief it is to perceive one's small but important place in the universe with some accuracy! To be able to say to oneself, and believe it—here I am, small but growing, ignorant but learning, petty but achieving greater perspective, hostile and afraid but growing in love and confidence—is to be on the road to magnificent freedom. It is to do much to establish a new relation between teacher and student and between teacher and teacher. If I observe correctly, nearly all institutions of higher learning are seriously poisoned now by a web of pretense—an attempt to protect and sustain false notions of status and prestige which are rooted in meaningless pride. Probably large numbers of teachers long to escape this meaningless game and in reverence and humility grow from where they are. Here then is a profoundly rewarding avenue for personality growth through teaching.

6. Peace. When peace is suggested as a crucial component of a healing growth, a fundamental question arises, Is not peace

in contradiction to the dynamic quality which is the essence of growth? Peace as the term is used here is at the very core of optimum growth. In the deepest sense, it is both the end and the means of growth.

The basic concept has been suggested by the last chapter of Professor Whitehead's great book, *Adventures of Ideas*.[7] In Part III of that book he analyzes the qualities which are fundamental to civilization: Truth, Beauty, Adventure, Art, Peace. In the last chapter he undertakes to tie his thoughts about man's progress in civilization together under the title of peace.

It is essentially a philosophy of life that gives unity and meaning to the search and struggle. Such peace is not political peace or even lack of tension between persons. It arises from an individual's basic beliefs—what he holds to be true. It is a result of the complex of ideas, feelings, and beliefs by which a man lives. Although there is a certain quality of quiet about this peace, it is the most fully living thing in all the world for it makes the fullest unfolding life possible. It becomes a core of stability from which never-ending growth flows.

There are many examples of this quality in the history of man, but let us think here of only two, the two that have most profoundly influenced the development of the best in Western civilization: Socrates of Athens and Jesus of Nazareth. A little book called *Socrates: The Man and His Thought*, written by Alfred Taylor,[8] would be helpful to any teacher interested in seeing the results of a unified philosophy by which to live. The Christian scriptures are everywhere available, but I fear often neglected and distorted. A growing teacher cannot afford to neglect them, and will find genuine study of them, free from distortion, an exercise of much profit and satisfaction. I have found special pleasure in *The New English Bible: New Testament*, a recent translation.[9]

The present world is full of fear, confusion, and tension. To a degree man's world has always been such, but many factors make current life more threatening and disturbing than ever before. We are suggesting that if the modern teacher would fulfill his privileges and responsibilities well he must be developing a body of principle by which he lives that progressively gives him the poise and strength of peace in the midst of great struggle. In short, he must be growing in peace if he would develop optimum personality (his own and his students') through teaching.

There is a danger that all of this will seem abstract and little related to life. What are some of the practical implications of growth in this quality?

A unified but ever growing philosophy of life assists one to learn the great lesson of acceptance—not the acceptance of despair or slavery or death, but that of hope, of freedom, and continuous rebirth. Through understanding, which perhaps approaches wisdom, the person learns to accept, and thus deal with creatively, the nature of himself, of others, and of the wider Universe. He thus may gradually escape the desperate scratching at life (including self, others, and the nature of things) that arises from fear and its evil child, hatred, and enter the province of satisfying growth. In this province there is struggle often of profound and far-reaching significance, but the personality's reaction to it is not fearful defense but self-fulfilling growth—a growth that instead of producing a steadily increasing weight of harmful armor frees and strengthens for the next encounter.

An important aspect of acceptance is some understanding of the nature and place of tragedy in human life. Many seem to confuse widespread misery and the various manifestations of man's inhumanity to man with the profound principle of tragedy. Misery and suffering often accompany tragedy, but they are in no sense its essence. The central meaning of tragedy lies in the gap between man's aspirations or dreams and his performance or accomplishments, and in his struggle to close this gap. He is forever dreaming—perhaps nothing is more fundamental to his nature—forever falling far short of his vision, and forever striving to come up to his dreams.

Clearly this process has built into it a kind of failure, for the vision always outruns the performance, however good the accomplishment. Thus, in a sense, every individual life and every organized society is a tragedy; but in this process seems to lie the source of man's creativeness. Of course the struggle is often small and petty and manifests little of the classic quality which is so related to potential-releasing growth. Indeed, as we have tried to show, the teacher's attempt to deal with this tragic aspect of life all too frequently results in a web of ineffective and unattractive personality traits. Some understanding and acceptance of the tragic nature which includes profound creative promise is of great value to the teacher.

A coherent philosophy places one's life in a framework infinitely larger than himself. The growing person puts his life in an ever-extending frame of place, time, and thought. Spinoza suggested that the best character is set in a framework of eternity. In this way the individual life escapes the petty limitations of its narrowly personal concerns and achieves some unity with larger and more meaningful concerns of man and God.

One of the greatest evils of man is unwholesome self-reference. The theme of most of the great teachers of mankind has been the need of a growth beyond self. This long-time view is of special importance to the person who aspires to greatness in teaching. The most important aspects of the teacher's work reach far beyond the immediate into the long continuous processes of generations. Much of the best he achieves appears too late for him to see; thus he rarely is overtly commended or rewarded for his efforts. History more often shows him neglected, misunderstood, and not infrequently done to death.

One illustration on the positive side makes the nature and power of the long view clearer. Some years ago I went back to visit on a farm in my home community. My friend who owned the small farm was now old—in his early 80's—and not very well. I found him working along a fence line behind the old house. After a brief greeting, I inquired what he was doing. He was planting young apple trees. As the mind will do, in a twinkling my mind surveyed the situation: an old man even now short of breath from a heart ailment; family grown and gone, uninterested in the farm that nourished and supported their education; very young apple trees that at best would not bear fruit for many years. Evidently this man could not enjoy or even see the fruit of this afternoon's labor.

Of course I did not raise this question. But he sensed my thought and said that it was his chief joy to plant for tomorrow. The satisfaction did not seem to flow from an anticipation of anything that might come to him or his family now or later, but chiefly from a widely based concern for the enrichment and betterment of life in all its varied manifestations. Certainly my farmer friend would not have expressed his feeling and faith so formally, but the crucial sense of the ongoing nature of life and his vital role in it apart from self-centered preoccupations was there. A great teacher needs something of this conception of life.

The peace of which we speak is a great support for a faith that gives meaning and zest to the living of life. To believe deeply that life is worthwhile one must believe in himself, in others, and in the ultimate goodness of the large processes of the Universe. Without such faith the entire process tends to become a painful, meaningless, losing struggle. At the end of Hamlet's speech on the magnificent qualities of men, quoted earlier, he concludes, "And yet, to me, what is this quintessence of dust? man delights not me; no, nor woman neither, though by your smiling you seem to say so." Or a self-destroyed Macbeth describes life as being, "a tale told by an idiot, full of sound and fury, signifying nothing."

There is an interesting passage in *The Return of the Native*, by the English novelist, Thomas Hardy, that describes the loss of a zest for life:

In Clym Yeobright's face could be dimly seen the typical countenance of the future. Should there be a classic period to art hereafter, its Pheidias may produce such faces. The view of life as a thing to be put up with, replacing that zest for existence which was so intense in early civilizations, must ultimately enter so thoroughly into the constitution of the advanced races that its facial expression will become accepted as a new artistic departure.[10]

The loss of this basic belief in life, this zest for life, this faith in its significance often results in a panic of activity designed to deceive oneself and others by pretending almost violently that life is good and meaningful. Caught in this trap the individual pursues all the empty symbols so publicized in our time: sophistication, material accoutrements, conformity, activity, status, tawdry honors. Pretense may be built mountain high, but the self remains empty, directionless, and anxious.

The teacher who would grow through teaching must cultivate the roots of peace—a philosophy of life based upon the fullest truth he can perceive. He will be growing in the ability to look squarely at every part of life, particularly its tragic nature, and yet be inspired and challenged by its processes and its promise for the gradual fulfillment and enrichment of human life.

So we come, for the moment, to the end of our thoughts together about the relation of teaching to personality development. Teachers will know that these thoughts are merely hints of what might be said, and also only the suggestions of one fellow-teacher whose sole claim to authority is that he is a searcher after truth and wisdom. The hope is that other thoughts will be stirred and a more widespread search stimulated.

The thesis of this chapter is not that every teacher must be a *great* teacher or a *great* person in order to achieve full personality development through teaching or to avoid serious personality damage. The central idea is that the teacher must be *growing toward* excellence in every phase of his life that relates to teaching. An increasingly clear vision of the goal and a steady growth toward it do not seem beyond reasonable hope. In such growth lie the promise of protection against serious harm and the fullest realization of the teacher as a person.

One final observation. The goals set for teaching in this book may seem to many of us discouragingly high, but in honesty we cannot describe a vision as any less than what we see.

Books Fellow Teachers Have Enjoyed and Found Helpful

Earl V. Pullias
Aileene Lockhart

ASSOCIATION FOR SUPERVISION AND CURRICULUM DEVELOPMENT. *Perceiving, Behaving, Becoming.* Washington, D. C.: National Education Association, 1962.

ATKINSON, BROOKS (ED.). *College in a Yard.* Cambridge: Harvard University Press, 1958.

BOWRA, C. M. *The Greek Experience.* Cleveland, Ohio: The World Publishing Company, 1957.

BRUNER, JEROME S. *The Process of Education.* Cambridge: Harvard University Press, 1961.

————. *On Knowing: Essays for the Left Hand.* Cambridge: Harvard University Press, 1962.

BRYSON, LYMAN. *The Drive Toward Reason.* New York: Harper and Brothers, 1954.

COOPER, RUSSELL M. (ED.). *The Two Ends of the Log.* Minneapolis: University of Minnesota Press, 1958.

COX, SIDNEY. *A Swinger of Birches.* New York: New York University Press, 1957.

DIMNET, ERNEST. *The Art of Thinking.* New York: Premier Books, 1957.

EDDY, EDWARD D., JR. *The College Influence on Student Character.* Washington, D. C.: American Council on Education, 1959.

EISELEY, LOREN. *The Mind as Nature.* New York: Harper and Row, 1962.

FROMM, ERICH. *The Art of Loving.* New York: Harper and Brothers, 1956.

GARDNER, JOHN. *Excellence.* New York: Harper and Brothers, 1961.

GARRISON, ROGER H. *The Adventure of Learning in College.* New York: Harper and Brothers, 1959.

GHISELIN, BREWSTER (ED.). *The Creative Process*. New York: Mentor Books, 1955.

HAMILTON, EDITH. *The Echo of Greece*. New York: W. W. Norton and Company, Inc., 1957.

HIGHET, GILBERT. *The Art of Teaching*. New York: Alfred A. Knopf, Inc., 1950.

HOCKING, W. E. *The Coming World Civilization*. New York: Harper and Brothers, 1956.

HUTCHINS, ROBERT M. *Freedom, Education, and the Fund*. Meridian Books, No. 31, 1956.

JAMES, WILLIAM. *Talks to Teachers and Other Essays*. New York: Henry Holt and Company, 1925.

JASPERS, KARL. *The Idea of the University*. Boston: Beacon Press, 1959.

JERSILD, A. *When Teachers Face Themselves*. New York: Teachers College, Columbia University, Bureau of Publications, 1955.

KELLER, HELEN. *Teacher: Anne Sullivan Macy*. Garden City, New York: Doubleday & Co., Inc., 1955.

LAO-TZU. *Tao Teh King*. Interpreted as Nature and Intelligence by Archie J. Bahm. New York: Frederick Ungar Publishing Company, 1958.

THE BOOK OF TAO. Translated by Frank J. MacHovec. Mt. Vernon, N. Y.: Peter Pauper Press, 1962.

MASLOW, A. H. *Motivation and Personality*. New York: Harper and Brothers, 1954.

————. *Toward a Psychology of Being*. Princeton, N. J.: D. Van Nostrand Company, Inc., 1962.

MURPHY, GARDNER. *Freeing Intelligence through Teaching*. New York: Harper and Brothers, 1961.

————. *Human Potentialities*. New York: Basic Books, Inc., 1958.

ORTEGA Y GASSET, JOSE. *Mission of the University*. London: Routledge and Kegan Paul, Ltd., 1946.

————. *The Revolt of the Masses*. New York: W. W. Norton and Company, Inc., 1932.

PARKES, HENRY B. *Gods and Men*. New York: Alfred A. Knopf, Inc., 1959.

PETERSON, HOUSTON. *Great Teachers*. New Brunswick, N. J.: Rutgers University Press, 1946.

ROGERS, CARL R. *On Becoming a Person*. Boston: Houghton Mifflin Company, 1961.

SCHWEITZER, ALBERT. *Out of My Life and Thought*. New York: Henry Holt and Company, 1933. Revised 1949.

SMITH, HUSTON. *Purposes of Higher Education*. New York: Harper and Brothers, 1955.

SMITH, LILLIAN. *The Journey*. Cleveland, Ohio: The World Publishing Co., 1954.

SNOW, C. P. *The Two Cultures and the Scientific Revolution.* New York: Cambridge University Press, 1960.

TAYLOR, HAROLD. *On Education and Freedom.* New York: Abelard-Schuman Limited, 1954.

TEAD, ORDWAY. *College Teaching and College Learning.* New Haven, Conn.: Yale University Press, 1949.

—————. *The Climate of Learning.* New York: Harper and Brothers, 1958.

TILLICH, PAUL. *The Courage to Be.* New Haven, Conn.: Yale University Press, 1953.

ULICH, ROBERT. *The Education of Nations.* Cambridge: Harvard University Press, 1961.

WHITEHEAD, A. N. *The Aims of Education.* New York: Macmillan, 1929.

—————. *Adventures of Ideas.* New York: Macmillan, 1933.

WILLIAMS, GEORGE. *Some of My Best Friends Are Professors.* New York: Abelard-Schuman Limited, 1958.

WISE, W. MAX. *They Come for the Best of Reasons.* Washington, D. C.: American Council on Education, 1958.

WRIGHT, AUSTIN TAPPAN. *Islandia.* New York: Farrar & Rinehart, 1942.

Bibliography

Chapter 1

1. JOSÉ ORTEGA Y GASSET, *Mission of the University*. London: Routledge and Kegan Paul, Ltd., 1946.
2. ARNOLD TOYNBEE in *Education in the Perspective of History* by Edward D. Myers with a concluding chapter by Arnold J. Toynbee. New York: Harper and Brothers, 1960.
3. JOHN S. BRUBACHER AND WILLIS RUDY, *Higher Education in Transition*. New York: Harper and Brothers, 1958.
   FREDERICK RUDOLPH, *The American College and University: A History*. New York: Alfred A. Knopf, 1962.
4. EDWARD D. EDDY, JR., *Colleges for Our Land and Time*. New York: Harper and Brothers, 1957.
5. BURTON R. CLARK, *The Open Door College*. New York: McGraw-Hill Book Co., 1960.
6. U. S. OFFICE OF EDUCATION, *Opening (Fall) Enrollment in Higher Education, 1960: Analytic Report*. Washington, D. C.: United States Government Printing Office, 1961.

Chapter 2

1. JOHN W. GARDNER, *Excellence*. New York: Harper and Brothers, 1961.
2. LOUIS T. BENEZET, "The Trouble with Excellence," *Saturday Review*, October 21, 1961.
3. EDITH HAMILTON, *The Echo of Greece*. New York: W. W. Norton & Co., 1957.
4. PHILIP E. JACOBS, *Changing Values in College*. New York: Harper and Brothers, 1957.
5. GEORGE WILLIAMS, *Some of My Best Friends Are Professors*. New York: Abelard-Schuman Ltd., 1958.

6. HOUSTON PETERSON, *Great Teachers.* New Brunswick, N. J.: Rutgers University Press, 1946.
7. GILBERT HIGHET, *The Art of Teaching.* New York: Alfred A. Knopf, Inc., 1950.
8. BROOKS ATKINSON (ED.), *College in a Yard.* Cambridge: Harvard University Press, 1958.
9. HELEN KELLER, *Teacher: Anne Sullivan Macy.* Garden City, N. Y.: Doubleday & Co., Inc., 1955.
10. RUSSELL M. COOPER (ED.), *The Two Ends of the Log.* Minneapolis: University of Minnesota Press, 1958.
11. ALFRED N. WHITEHEAD, *The Aims of Education.* New York: Macmillan Company, 1929. Reprinted by permission of the Macmillan Company.
12. GARDNER MURPHY, *Freeing Intelligence through Teaching.* New York: Harper and Brothers, 1961.

Chapter 3
1. SAMUEL ELIOT MORISON, *Three Centuries of Harvard.* Cambridge: Harvard University Press, 1946.
2. BROOKS ATKINSON (ED.), *College in a Yard.* Cambridge: Harvard University Press, 1958.
3. ORDWAY TEAD, *The Climate of Learning.* New York: Harper and Brothers, 1958.
4. HUGH HAWKINS, *Pioneer: A History of the Johns Hopkins University.* Ithaca, N. Y.: Cornell University Press, 1960.
5. LAO-TZU, *Tao Teh King.* Interpreted as Nature and Intelligence by Archie J. Bahm. New York: Frederick Ungar Publishing Company, 1958.
The Book of Tao. Translated by Frank J. MacHovec. Mt. Vernon, N. Y.: Peter Pauper Press, 1962.
6. E. V. PULLIAS, "A Professional Reading Shelf for College Faculties," *Improving College and University Teaching,* Vol. IX, No. 4 (Autumn, 1961).
7. MARY RENAULT, *The Bull from the Sea.* New York: Pantheon Books, 1962.
8. RICHARD HUGHES, *The Fox in the Attic.* New York: Harper and Brothers, 1961.

Chapter 4
1. BRUNO BETTELHEIM, "The Problem of Generations," *Daedalus* (Winter, 1962). Vol. 91, No. 1, of the Proceedings of the American Academy of Arts and Sciences.
2. W. MAX WISE, *They Come for the Best of Reasons.* Washington, D. C.: American Council on Education, 1958.
3. NEVITT SANFORD (ED.), *The American College.* New York: John Wiley and Sons, Inc., 1962.
4. C. M. BOWRA, *The Greek Experience.* Cleveland, Ohio: The World Publishing Co., 1957.

5. HENRY JAMES, *The Short Stories of Henry James*. New York: The Modern Library, 1948.
6. SIDNEY COX, *A Swinger of Birches*. New York: New York University Press, 1957. Reprinted by permission of the New York University Press.

Chapter 5

1. ARTHUR KUDNER, "Little Words," *Saturday Review*, April 14, 1962. Reprinted by permission of the Kudner Agency Inc., Mrs. Roswell L. Gilpatric, Leo Burnett, and *Saturday Review*.
2. JACQUES HADAMARD, *The Psychology of Invention in the Mathematical Field*. Princeton, New Jersey: Princeton University Press, 1945.
3. ISIDOR ISAAC RABI, "Men of the Year," *Time*, January 2, 1961. Reprinted by permission of *Time*.
4. ASHLEY MONTAGU, *The Cultured Man*. Cleveland, Ohio: World Publishing Company, 1958.
5. SUSAN STEBBING, *Thinking to Some Purpose*. Baltimore, Maryland: Penguin Books, 1959. Reprinted by permission of Penguin Books.
6. SUSAN STEBBING, *Ibid*. Reprinted by permission of Penguin Books.
7. SEYMOUR M. FARBER AND ROGER H. L. WILSON (ED.), *Control of the Mind*. New York: McGraw-Hill Book Co., 1961.
8. ERNEST DIMNET, *The Art of Thinking*. New York: Premier Books, 1952.

Chapter 6

1. J. P. GUILFORD, "The Nature of Creativity," Proceedings of the 1960 Summer Conference on "Intelligence, Creativity, and Learning." Bellingham, Washington: Western Washington College Bulletin, Vol. 13, No. 3, December, 1960.
2. J. P. GUILFORD, "Three Faces of Intellect," *American Psychologist*, 14:478, August, 1959. Reprinted by permission of American Psychological Association.
3. DONALD W. MACKINNON, "What Makes a Person Creative?" *Saturday Reveiw*, February 10, 1962. Reprinted by permission of *Saturday Review*.
4. WILLIAM F. BUCKLEY, JR., *Up From Liberalism*, New York: Hillman Periodicals, Inc., 1961. Reprinted by permission of Hillman Periodicals and William F. Buckley, Jr.
5. J. H. MCPHERSON, "A Proposal for Establishing Ultimate Criteria for measuring Creative Output," *The 1955 University of Utah Research Conference on the Identification of Creative Talent;* (C. W. Taylor, Editor) Salt Lake City: University of Utah Press, 1956.
6. JOHN W. GARDNER, *Excellence*. New York: Harper and Brothers, 1961. Reprinted by permission of Harper and Row.

7. JAMES WEBB YOUNG, *A Technique for Producing Ideas*. Chicago: Advertising Publications, Inc., 1953.
8. PAT MAIL, a student, University of Arizona, 1961.
9. IRVING A. TAYLOR, "Creativity Research for Future Creativity," *Implications of Creativity Research*. Proceedings of a Conference on "The Future Implications of Creativity Research"; co-sponsored by Los Angeles State College and Chouinard Art Institute. Los Angeles, March 10, 1962.

Chapter 7

1. CHARLES A. ROBINSON, "Alexander the Great and His Idea of One World," "Graduate Lecture Series: The Functions of Teaching," by Jerome S. Bruner. *Rhode Island College Journal*, March, 1960.
2. HENRY NELSON WIEMAN, *Man's Ultimate Commitment*. Carbondale, Illinois: Southern Illinois University Press, 1958. Reprinted by permission of Southern Illinois University Press.
3. ASSOCIATION FOR SUPERVISION AND CURRICULUM DEVELOPMENT, *Perceiving, Becoming, Behaving*, Washington, D. C.: National Education Association, 1962.
4. JEROME S. BRUNER, "Graduate Lecture Series: The Functions of Teaching," by Jerome S. Bruner. *Rhode Island College Journal*, March, 1960.
5. F. CHAMPION WARD, R. BRUCE LINDSAY, DAVID RIESMAN, THEODORE BRAMELD, EDWARD D. EDDY, JR., "Symposium: Modern Society's Challenge to Education," *Rhode Island College Journal*, December, 1959.

Chapter 8

1. CLYDE KLUCKHOLN *et al*, "Values and Value-Orientations in the Theory of Action," *Toward a General Theory of Action* (Talcott Parsons and Edward A. Shils, editors) Cambridge: Harvard University Press, 1951.
2. GORDON N. ALLPORT, *Patterns and Growth in Personality*. New York: Holt, Rinehart, and Winston, 1961.
3. DOUGLAS LAWSON, *Wisdom and Education*. Carbondale, Illinois: Southern Illinois University Press, 1961.
4. J. E. C. WELLDON, *The Nicomachean Ethics of Aristotle, Translated with an Analysis and Critical Notes*. New York: Macmillan Company, 1892.
5. JOHN PLAMENATZ, *Mill's Utilitarianism Reprinted With a Study of the English Utilitarians*. Oxford: Basil Blackwell and Mott Limited, 1949.
6. JOSÉ ORTEGA Y GASSETT, *Mission of the University*. Princeton, New Jersey: Princeton University Press, 1944. Reprinted by permission of Princeton University Press.

7. HUSTON SMITH, "Values: Academic and Human," *The Larger Learning* (Marjorie Carpenter, editor). Dubuque, Iowa: William C. Brown Company, 1960.

8. D. R. BROWN, "Non-Intellectual Qualities and the Perception of the Ideal Student by College Faculty," *The Journal of Educational Sociology*, 33, 1960. Reprinted by permission of *The Journal of Educational Sociology*.

9. CHRISTOPHER JENCKS, "The Next Thirty Years in College." *Harpers Magazine*, 223, 1961. Reprinted by permission of *Harpers Magazine*.

10. FREDERICK MAYER, *Creative Universities*. New Haven: College and University Press publications, 1961. Reprinted by permission of College and University Press.

11. NEVITT SANFORD (ED.), "Higher Education as a Social Problem," *The American College*. New York: John Wiley and Sons, Inc., 1962. Reprinted by permission of John Wiley and Sons, Inc.

12. THEODORE M. NEWCOMB, "Student Peer—Group Influence," *The American College* (ed. Nevitt Sanford) New York: John Wiley and Sons, Inc., 1962.

Chapter 9

1. A. JERSILD, *When Teachers Face Themselves*. New York: Columbia University, Teachers College, 1955.

2. A. H. MASLOW, *Motivation and Personality*. New York: Harper and Brothers, 1954.

3. ————. *Toward a Psychology of Being*. Princeton, N. J.: D. Van Nostrand Company, 1962.

4. GARDNER MURPHY, *Freeing Intelligence through Teaching*. New York: Harper and Brothers, 1961.

5. HANS SELYE, *The Stress of Life*. New York: McGraw-Hill Book Company, 1956.

6. FRANZ E. WINKLER, *Man: The Bridge Between Two Worlds*. New York: Harper and Brothers, 1960.

7. ALDOUS HUXLEY, *The Perennial Philosophy*. New York: Harper and Brothers, 1945.

8. PAUL TILLICH, *The Dynamics of Faith*. New York: Harper and Brothers, 1957.

9. CRANE BRINTON, *Ideas and Men: The Story of Western Thought*. Englewood Cliffs, N. J.: Prentice-Hall, Inc., 1950.

10. LEWIS CAMPBELL (TRANS.), *Sophocles: The Seven Plays in English Verse*. London: Oxford University Press, 1906.

Chapter 10

1. EDNA ST. VINCENT MILLAY, *Collected Poems*. New York: Harper and Brothers, Copyright 1912, 1940, 1956 by Edna St. Vincent Millay. Permission by Norma Millay Ellis.

2. RICHARD HUGHES, *The Fox in the Attic*. New York: Harper and Brothers, 1961.
3. LILLIAN SMITH, *The Journey*. Cleveland, Ohio: The World Publishing Co., 1954.
4. NIKOS KAZANTZAKIS, *The Saviors of God: Spiritual Exercises*. Translated with an Introduction by Kimon Friar. New York: Simon & Schuster, 1960.
5. EDITH HAMILTON, *The Echo of Greece*. New York: W. W. Norton and Company, Inc., 1957.
6. A. N. WHITEHEAD, *The Aims of Education*. New York: Macmillan, 1929. Reprinted by permission of the Macmillan Company.
7. ———. *Adventures of Ideas*. New York: The New American Library of World Literature, 1955.
8. ALFRED E. TAYLOR, *Socrates: The Man and His Thought*. New York: Doubleday & Co., 1933.
9. *The New English Bible: New Testament*, Oxford University Press-Cambridge University Press, 1961.
10. THOMAS HARDY, *The Return of the Native*. London: Macmillan and Co., Limited, 1933. Reprinted by permission of Macmillan and Company.